Emma, We Love You

Emma, We Love You

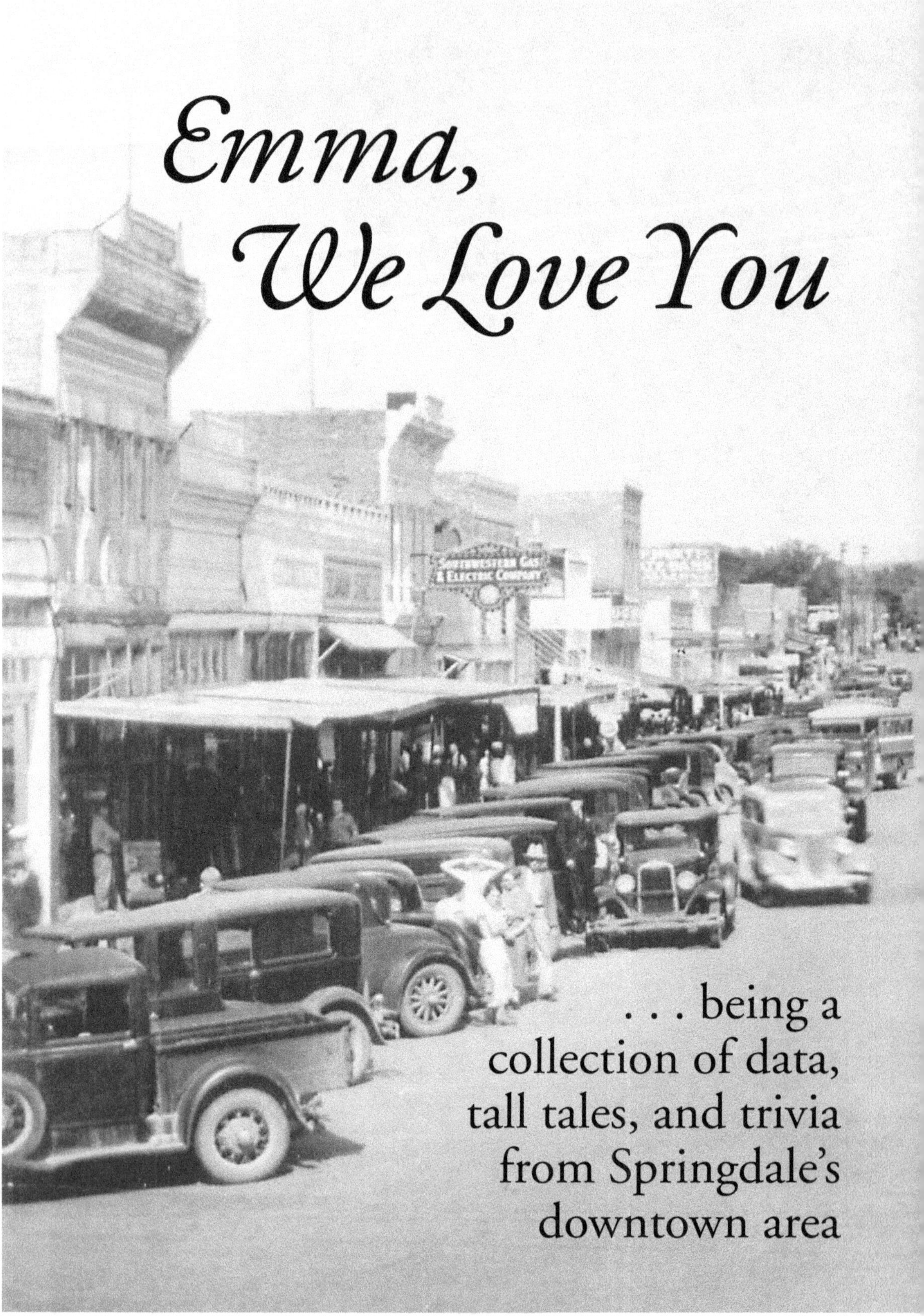

. . . being a
collection of data,
tall tales, and trivia
from Springdale's
downtown area

BY BRUCE VAUGHAN

SHILOH MUSEUM
OF OZARK HISTORY

Springdale, Arkansas 1994

3rd Edition, Revised
ISBN: 978-0-98973-627-5

Designed by Liz Lester

Emma, We Love You and *Twenty-three Skidoo*
By Bruce Vaughan
and copies of photographs used in this book may be purchased from:

Shiloh Museum of Ozark History
118 W. Johnson Avenue
Springdale, AR 72764

This is the land of lost content,
I see it shining plain,
The happy highways where I went
And cannot go again.

A. E. HOUSMAN
1859–1936

DEDICATION

This book is respectfully dedicated to all merchants of Emma Avenue—both past and present.

Today Emma continues, strong and vital to our community. While the downtown economy has moved from retail sales to financial and professional services, the "Main Street of Northwest Arkansas" is still here. Emma's health is good; her prognosis is excellent.

—B. V.

FOREWORD

Emma Avenue has always been the heart of Springdale.

Once that heart beat strongly in the breast of a thriving town. Like so many small communities in the 1920s and 1930s, Springdale bustled with activity—most of it along a few blocks of Emma Avenue. Small trucks bringing strawberries to market; big trucks hauling freight for the fledging Jones Truck Line; families shopping and socializing at the movie houses and drug stores on Saturday night. Even the seedy side of Springdale seemed to congregate along a short stretch of Emma Avenue, sometimes punctuating the usual peaceful atmosphere of the community with moments of violence.

In the following chapters, long-time businessman Bruce Vaughan recounts his memories of growing up in Springdale. Vaughan uses an effective blend of personal anecdotes and interviews with other "old timers" to recall those sometimes difficult years when electricity, cars, and radios were beginning to change the very fabric of rural American life.

Like so many other early Springdale residents, Vaughan's youth centered around Emma Avenue and the small, struggling businesses that kept the town's economy alive.

Vaughan's trip along Emma Avenue is in two parts: Before and after World War II. When the United States entered the war in December 1941, he joined the exodus of young men to the military, serving in the Air Corps. He returned in 1945 to an uncertain future. After a brief period at the University of Arkansas, Vaughan made a decision that defined the rest of his life. He quit college and, utilizing his wartime training, opened a radio shop . . . on Emma Avenue, of course.

Vaughan also writes from a unique perspective. He helped pioneer radio in Springdale and he brought the first television to the growing post-war community. Chapter 5 recounts those days of snowy, black and white televison. And, in an appendix, he recounts the history of radio in Northwest Arkansas.

Ultimately, a flood in 1950 (Chapter 7), a growing population, and changes brought by Urban Renewal caused some merchants, including Vaughan, to leave Emma Avenue and join a burgeoning business community along Highway 71.

The 1960s and 1970s drastically altered the economic makeup of Emma Avenue as the business community spread out along Highway 71 and Highway 68 (now U.S. 412), and in subsequent years the downtown area suffered through periods of decline and vacant storefronts. Today, as Springdale moves into a new century, people who still value Emma Avenue are working to strengthen the city's heart. But, as Vaughan concludes, an era that helped push Springdale toward prosperity, an era that provokes nostalgia about those "good old days" of small-town America—is gone forever. The heartbeat of Emma Avenue will never be as strong.

—JIM MORRISS, JANUARY 2004
Retired editor of *The Morning News of Northwest Arkansas*

ACKNOWLEDGEMENTS

The list of people who contributed to the writing of this book is long. Help ranged from those who offered information on one small item, to those who consented to taped interviews.

I especially want to thank Bob Besom, Betty Bowling, Mary Brennan, Mary Parsons, Carolyn Reno, Manon Wilson, Susan Young, and Arie Poldevaart of the Shiloh Museum of Ozark History. Their daily assistance made publication of my book possible.

Thanks go to Liz Lester for her talent in layout and production, and for caring about the book.

All photographs used in the book are from the Mary D. Parsons Photograph Collection at the Shiloh Museum. Photographers who have donated their negative files to the museum include Howard Clark, Ray Watson, and Mary Vaughan. The photographs made by Charles Bickford, with *The Morning News,* were especially helpful in validating the exact locations of business firms.

I would like to thank Maudine Sanders for the proof reading and Mary Parsons for coordinating the preparation of the manuscript for printing.

The following taped interviews were of tremendous help: Bill Bailey, Tom Bain, Reuben Bryant, Bob Clark, Morris Clarkson, Curtis Hornor, Harry Howell, Mary Lawrence, Garvin Martini, Roy Nixon, Clifford Samuel, Mary Sellers, Mrs. Marty "Bucket" Stafford, and Espen Walters. Tapes of those interviews will be on file in the museum for future reference.

Bob Boyle and Ray Watson passed away before seeing my book published. Bob's story about Springdale's first airplane and Ray's story about Jones Truck Lines add much to the completed work. Thanks, old friends.

Finally, I thank my wife Mary, who has tolerated and encouraged my literary efforts. During the past two years I have been in front of my word processor more than by her side.

I sincerely hope the final result does justice to all the support I have enjoyed.

—B. V.

CONTENTS

*Numbers in text (i.e. #42) refer to location of buildings
on Maps, Emma Avenue, Plates 1–9*

PREFACE

Television changed the way America lived and thought. Few inventions, including the automobile, radio, and computer, have had more impact on a people.

It occurred to me that a book documenting the evolution of television from an expensive toy found in very few Northwest Arkansas homes to a common household necessity would be of interest to many. I was the first TV dealer in Springdale. To the best of my knowledge, I was the first TV dealer in Arkansas. When I purchased my seven-inch Hallicrafters—the third TV set in the state—my chances of seeing a picture ranged from poor to none at all. I therefore feel well-qualified to tell of the problems, frustrations, and misconceptions of this new form of entertainment.

As I began writing about my small radio shop on East Emma Avenue in Springdale, Arkansas, I became increasingly aware that every household—indeed, every individual in our city—was in many ways dependent on this one street. Our clothing, food, automobiles, health care, appearance, banking, insurance, recreation, and entertainment were inexorably tied to Emma Avenue. The busy street reminded me of the hub of a wheel, its spokes radiating outward to every household in our city. I'm sure the analogy has occurred to others. Some seventy years ago, one of Emma's better-known stores was named "The Hub."

This, then, is a story of the television age coming to Springdale. I hope I have captured some of the feelings, as well as bits of history, of the post-war years in downtown Springdale. Though my intentions were to concentrate on the immediate post-war period, an occasional excursion in time, forward and backward, became irresistible.

The early years of television were unique. The gestation periods of the computer and the automobile, for example, were much shorter than that of television. Television was demonstrated in the mid-1920s, some forty years after Nipkow invented the scanning disc, but it was not until Friday, June 10, 1949, that a TV picture was received in Northwest Arkansas. On the following Monday, *The Springdale News* printed this column:

VAUGHAN PICKS UP FIRST TELEVISION PROGRAMS HERE

Springdale received its first television show last night.

Bruce Vaughan Jr., operator of Electric Shop here and an avid radio and TV fan, received three programs from an Oklahoma City station which is over 200 miles.

"There was an amateur show, a symphony and a drama," Vaughan said, "and all came in fairly well."

Vaughan has what is believed to be the only television set in the Springdale area. It represents an investment of some $400 and a lot of hard work. He has an aerial that reaches a height of 60 feet.

According to Vaughan, Springdale and this particular area are not ready for television at the present time because of the great distance to the nearest station. However, with Tulsa scheduled to open a station soon, Vaughan believes Springdale will be able to have good reception on television by this winter.

Yes, television came to Springdale, snowy though it was. As the art of television progressed, my business grew accordingly. It was a frustrating experience, both for me and for those few forward-thinking individuals willing to invest hundreds of dollars in a primitive, cantankerous, and expensive-to-maintain gadget. Without the support of such individuals, not one of our complex inventions—those we deem necessary for our existence today—would ever have made it out of the laboratory and into general use.

I am not sure there is any accurate way to research Emma's business district, arriving at exact dates and locations. This book is the result of five years of research, forty years as a businessman in Springdale, and sixty years of living within three blocks of Emma; still, errors are bound to occur.

As an example, I opened my shop in early 1946; I have been unable to verify the exact day. For use in this book I chose a date based on my memory. I secured my sales tax permit very early, but not before opening my shop. Many others were equally lax in their paperwork. They chose to open up a business, try to turn a profit, and then get on the city, county, and state records.

You will notice that I have not concentrated on our larger business enterprises, but rather on people. This is intentional. Firms like Jones Truck Lines, George's, and Tyson's are well-documented. Little would be gained by repeating information that is well-known and readily available. However, there are small bits of information, considered unimportant by some, that disappear quickly.

Eyewitness accounts have served as my best source of material. While they may sometimes miss a date by a year or so, the stories they tell are of value. Stories about people who lived and worked along Emma Avenue should not be forgotten.

It is of prime importance that we preserve a few of those stories: stories that tell something of our past and stories that help us understand the characters and personalities of the men and women who made Springdale "The Main Street of Northwest Arkansas."

Bruce Vaughan
504 Maple Drive
Springdale, AR 72764
501–751–6536

CHAPTER I

This, Then, Was Emma

When our first parents were driven out of Paradise, Adam is believed to have remarked to Eve, "My dear, we live in an age of transition."

W. R. INGE (1860–1954)
DEAN OF ST. PAUL'S, LONDON

On a recent Saturday, late in the afternoon, I drove down Emma Avenue. Only three cars were parked between the old post office building and the railroad tracks. I parked in front of the First State—oops!—Worthen Bank. Looking across the street, I tried to remember where my old store had been located; it looks so different now.

In the distance a northbound train sounded its whistle as it approached the Caudle Street crossing. How similar, yet so very different, was the sound of the old Frisco steam locomotives! Steam whistles produced a melodic sound unattainable by other warning devices. Sitting there alone, I watched as the late afternoon light changed from yellow to gold, then gradually surrendered to darkness. My automobile became a time machine, as I recalled events from years ago, sharp and clear as if they had occurred yesterday.

APRIL 1940 . . .

I walked toward the Concord Theater, passing cars parked in front of the Pioneer. The old lumber company was one of the few business firms along Emma that did not stay open Saturday nights. Parking spaces on Emma Avenue did not remain vacant; they were soon filled by the Saturday night movie crowd.

Tradition dictated that the Concord and our new theater, the Shilo, feature western movies Friday nights, Saturday afternoons, and Saturday nights. Normally, these were class "B" westerns with William Boyd (Hop-along Cassidy), Ken Maynard, or Buck Jones. Tonight was different. They were showing John Ford's latest film, *Stagecoach*. It starred John Wayne in his first major western. Good reviews, no doubt, contributed to the overflow crowd.

ROBERT "BOB" H. CLARK (OCTOBER 1993)

. . . I forget the exact year, but it was about 1911—I remember I was about six years old—when someone put a movie theater in the building on the corner of Main and Emma (#27).

I remember going downtown one Saturday afternoon. I passed along the west side of the building, and the side door was open. The theater was unbearably hot for the Saturday matinee. Anyway, the door was open, and I stuck my head in to see what was showing. They had a movie newsreel going, showing scenes related to the sinking of the Titanic.

Some years later, Albert "Acme" Hough became the projectionist for the Concord Theater. This was in the 1920s. Acme and I were good friends; we were both interested in anything electrical. So I spent a lot of time with him in the projection room.

Well, some people from Huntsville came over to see him. They wanted to know if Acme would come to Huntsville once a week to show movies, provided they could raise the money to buy a machine.

Acme told them he would be glad to come. All they had to do was find a suitable building and buy a projector and screen. Somehow, they came into possession of a antique 35mm movie outfit.

He talked me into going along as his assistant. I can't remember the name of the church building we used, but it was near town and on the north side of Highway 68. (This sounds like the old First Methodist Church. I lived directly across the road from it in 1932—Author.)

We had no electricity in the church, so one of the Huntsville group provided a Fordson tractor. We jacked up the rear of the tractor and used the power take-off to drive a DC generator for the arc light in the movie machine. It was hand-cranked, of course. That's why Acme needed an assistant. I only made three or four trips. Dad decided I needed to spend my nights on my college studies.

ALBERT "ACME" HOUGH (1965)

When I went to work at the Concord, both our old projectors were cranked by hand.

I used to crank them at about the right speed for the first show. If only a few showed up for the second show, I really cranked the film through the machine. Those horses sure did run fast. I could crank a one hour movie through the projector in 45 minutes.

Later the owner bought a pair of Powers 6-B projectors. These were the workhorses of small theaters all over the country.

When sound movies came out in 1928–29, Powers made an attachment that could be added to their 6-Bs, making them full optical sound. I converted both machines. They continued to run for several more years.

I passed by the Concord Theater (how good the popcorn smelled!) and strolled toward Penrod's. Howard Clark waved as I walked past the window of the Clark-Deaver Hardware Company. He was demonstrating a small RCA radio to a young couple. Radio was one of their better-selling items.

Lee Gibson and an elderly gentleman came out of Oklahoma Tire. Lee was carrying a battery tester. I watched as they raised the hood of a '34 Chevrolet sedan. After testing the battery, Lee explained to the customer that it had a dead cell. It appeared Cecil Brown was about to sell another car battery.

As I approached the business "hub," that two-block area of Emma between Holcomb and Spring streets, sidewalk traffic became more congested. Some shoppers hurried by, carrying paper bags filled with recent purchases. Here and there, friends and neighbors gathered in small groups, visiting and passing time, until their families were ready to go home. Odors of hamburgers cooking, hot buttered popcorn, a cacophony of sounds, dozens of brightly lighted stores, and happy crowds of people bestowed a carnival-like aura on our downtown shopping area.

Lichlyter's, The Cash, Oklahoma Tire, The Famous, Palace Barber Shop, Wilson's, Clark-Deaver Hardware, Applegate's, Joyce's, Coger's, Myers' Dime Store, Penrod's, The Minit Inn, and Martini's Arkansas Brokerage Company drew business to dozens of smaller shops and stores within this downtown area. As you travelled west past The Famous or east past the tracks, foot traffic became more sporadic.

Traffic in a never-ending stream chugged slowly up the busy street, drivers looking for parking spaces. Finding none, cars made a "U" turn at the railroad tracks. Sometimes several trips between the railroad and the "U" turn at Shiloh and Emma proved fruitless. Eventually, most drivers gave up and settled for side street parking.

In the late 1940s, our city reluctantly eliminated the traditional "U" turns from Emma. Soon afterward, the city installed stop lights at Spring and at Holcomb. A shortage of parking spaces remained. There was talk of off-the-street parking lots, but little came of it.

Our city fathers, searching for an answer to downtown traffic congestion, voted to install parking meters. The decision appeared to be a good one. Unfortunately, it was an idea whose time had passed. Installation of the meters coincided with the beginning of the migration of business firms to outlying areas, namely Highway 71.

When retail customers began leaving the downtown area to shop on the highway, some thought it was because of the parking fee. The city council agreed, and our parking meters were removed. The return of free parking did little to increase downtown business. The shift in business from downtown areas to the suburbs was occurring all over America. In retrospect, there are things that might have slowed the migration, but nothing would have stopped it. Now, there was little need for stop lights at Holcomb and Spring; they, too, were removed.

Families often came to town early Saturday, spent the day, and returned home late that night. The entire family enjoyed looking in the stores, eating in one of the restaurants, taking in the Saturday afternoon matinee at the Concord, or just sitting in the car watching the sights.

Those who wished to avoid the sight of violence and bloodshed knew it was wise to avoid those parking spaces on the north side of Emma between Spring Street and the Frisco tracks. Few Saturdays passed without one or more angry confrontations. Often these differences of opinion led to a fist fight among some of our "hell raisers." I would not say that all of Springdale's sin was concentrated in this one block. However, a number of earthly pleasures—both legal and illegal, and not available in other sections of our fair city—were found here in abundance.

"Curb service," a custom originating in the early 1900s, was nearing its end. Those lucky enough to find parking in front of Joyce's, Coger's, or Applegate's drug store could still enjoy a fountain drink in the comfort of their cars. A short toot of the car horn would bring a young man running to take orders for five-cent cokes, fifteen and twenty-cent milk shakes and sundaes.

Rising labor costs, plus a shortage of parking spaces in front of downtown drug stores, spelled doom for this custom, relegating in-car service to a few drive-ins, which catered mostly to those too young to vote.

TOM BAIN (March 1994)

If you remember, Mr. Coger was in the hospital for quite some time before he died. Clifford (Samuel) visited him several times a day, trying to make his last days as pleasant as possible.

One morning when Clifford went in his room, it was obvious the elderly gentleman had had a bad night.

"Are you feeling worse, Mr. Coger?" asked Clifford. Coger replied, "I had a terrible, terrible dream last night, Clifford. I dreamed I died and went to hell. Just look at my feet; they are in a terrible shape. Clifford, it was a bad place. It was awful!"

"I'm sorry, Mr. Coger," answered Clifford. "It was just a dream."

"Clifford, I want to tell you something. You can't imagine how many Springdale folks I saw there. The place was full of people we know."

———

I've got another druggist story you might like . . .

When I lived up on Wayland Street, my neighbor was Chris Ahlschewede.

In the winter time Chris wore a small bag of asafetida tied around his neck to ward off colds and flu.

One day he went over to Jim Oglesby's Drug Store. "Jim," said Chris, "give me a dime's worth of asafetida."

Jim went in the back of his store, returning a few minutes later with a small pill box full of the smelly medicinal plant. Chris felt in his hip pocket and discovered he had left his billfold at home. Then he went through his pockets. They were empty also . . .

"Just put it on my account, Jim," said Chris. "I'll take care of it at the end of the month."

Jim got a charge pad and started to write. He looked puzzled. Then he said, "Tell you what, Chris. I'll just give you the darn medicine. I wouldn't spell Ahlschewede or asafetida for twenty-five cents a word."

Nine o'clock was closing time for retail stores. Drug stores and restaurants remained open until around eleven. Those who got off work at 9:00 P.M. and movie patrons—thirsty after eating two bags of salty popcorn—often stopped in for cold drinks, coffee, or a late night snack.

MAY 1941 . . .

It has been a good year for strawberries. Most growers seem to think the good picking might last another week to ten days.

I look at my wrist watch. Only 2:30 P.M., and already Emma traffic is blocked from Spring Street to well past Clarkson's on the east. The traffic jam will peak about 4:30 P.M. as growers, their patches picked clean for the day, bring their bright red berries to town. Pickup trucks, overloaded cars, and even an occasional horse-drawn wagon converge on the area near the tracks. Buyers, waiting along the curb, descend upon each loaded vehicle before it stops rolling.

Buyers are easily identified; each has a small, shiny berry crate tool in his hip pocket. After prying the lid from a berry crate, buyers make their offer.

"Three dollars and a dime. I'll take 'em all."

Every grower knows better than to take the first offer. By now, three or four other buyers are looking at his berries.

"Three dollars and fifteen cents!" yells another buyer.

"Tell you what," says the first buyer. "I'll go three twenty-five . . . and that's my final offer."

The other three buyers, shocked by the ten cent per crate jump in price, turn and walk away.

The grower is left with only one buyer and decides to sell his load.

On occasion, the growers' vehicles became surrounded by other loaded trucks. Unable to move a load of produce, the seller and buyer worked together, carrying the crates by hand to one of the railside sheds. Within hours, another train load of Arkansas strawberries was on its way north to big city markets.

Prosperity was a word, not a state of being, for most folks in the 1930s. The purchase of long-desired luxuries became possible when strawberry crops were good. A luxury in the '30s was anything you could live without.

Young and old alike bent their backs in the rocky strawberry patches of Northwest Arkansas. In 1932, growers paid from two to three cents a quart to get their berries picked. By the late 1930s times were getting better. A good berry picker could make four to five dollars a day, possibly as much as $75 during the season. A large portion of this easy (easy?) money was spent with the area merchants. The only season better than strawberry time was Christmas.

What would this strawberry money buy? Well, in a 1940 issue of *The Springdale News,* The Cash was advertising overalls for $1.19. At the Springdale Meat Market, spareribs cost twenty cents a pound. Large dill pickles were five cents each; sweet pickles went for twenty cents a dozen. Late Chevrolet sold Chevrolet sedans for $610 and one-and-a-half ton trucks for about $800. A good wool suit might run as much as $20. Stores had a lot of good shoes for under $4 a pair. A nice RCA radio cost $20, and new Frigidaire refrigerators ran from $75 to $100. Washing machines started around $40, and a $10 bill would buy a Remington or Winchester single-shot rifle—excellent used ones, much less.

> *Living in the past has one thing in its favor—it's cheaper.*
> ANONYMOUS

SUMMER 1938 . . .

That section of Mill Street, just north of Emma and between Wilson's and the First National Bank, might well be considered the heart of downtown Springdale. Pitchmen, hucksters, curbside medicine shows, itinerant preachers—even our downtown merchants' association—found the location ideal. I enjoyed the hucksters and pitchmen most of all.

I was standing in front of Penrod's when the old Pontiac sedan came down Emma, turned north, and parked near the west door of Wilson's Mercantile.

A dark-complexioned man, about forty years old, stepped from the car. From under a worn cowboy hat two long braids of black hair fell forward, reaching below the pockets of his faded denim shirt. Inside the car, I could see an attractive dark-skinned young lady.

Stepping to the trunk of the car, the man rummaged through a pile of junk. He removed an old rusty cow bell which he began ringing as he paced back and forth across the dirt street. It had the desired effect.

A sizeable crowd quickly assembled to see what all the commotion was about. The young lady stepped from the car, receiving more than a few appreciative glances. So far, neither she nor the "Indian" had spoken a word.

Suddenly the ringing stopped. Walking to the open trunk of the Pontiac, the "Indian" removed a water bucket, a old #2 wash tub, and a huge sandstone rock. He placed them on the ground in front of the crowd, then spoke for the first time.

"Where can I get some water?" he asked.

"There's a tap over by the bank," one on-looker replied. "They use it fer washin' their winders."

The man carried five or six buckets of water from the bank, pouring them in the tub. When it was half full, he put the bucket on the ground.

"I am going to show you something today you will never see again," he said. "I am going to drink this entire tub of water. After filling my stomach to the bursting point, I will beat this rock into sand, using nothing but my bare fist. I know you will never in this life have a chance to see anything like this again. Most people would give a ten-dollar bill to see a sight like this. My wife is going to pass my hat among you. I know you can't expect to see this for nothing."

The young lady passed the hat among the crowd, then returned to her husband. He glanced down at the nickels, dimes, and quarters. Obviously, from the frown on his face, he was disappointed.

"Pass the hat again," he said. "Surely this fine bunch of people don't expect to see one of the most amazing feats in history for a few nickels and dimes. Just think of the torture my body will undergo as I drink this entire tub of water. You can see that my bladder will have to swell to a size unknown to medical science. Then with my poor distorted body suffering terrible pain, I am going to pound this rock into sand with my bare fist. Surely a few among you are willing to put some folding money in my hat."

Again the young lady passed among the gullible crowd. This time a few dropped a dollar bill into the hat. She handed the hat to her companion.

"I simply don't believe this," he said. "I am going to ask my wife to pass my hat around again. This time act like you want to see one of the most amazing miracles of the twentieth century. This is something you can tell your children and grandchildren about."

The young lady passed among the crowd slowly, holding the old beat-up Stetson in front of every man there. With a demure smile, she asked in a soft voice, "Please, sir." Several bills went into the hat this round, but it was obvious the crowd was getting restless. She returned the hat to her accomplice, walked slowly around the Pontiac, and got in.

The man looked in the hat, frowned, and shook his head from side to side. Then he said, "It's plain to see that you people don't give a damn whether you see my act or not."

So saying, he plopped the hat on his head (the money still inside), jumped into his car, hit the starter, and disappeared down Mill Street in a cloud of dust, leaving his bucket and rusty tub of water in the middle of the street.

Yes, all the tricks and cons were worked here in the Depression years: three card monte, the burned match ruse, pills that charged auto batteries, automobile ignition boosters that increased mileage, and, of course, miraculous cures for everything from cancer to "nervous spells."

It was considered entertainment; I never knew anyone to be arrested. Most of us took our loss with a smile, too ashamed or embarrassed to complain.

> *It was beautiful and simple, as all truly great swindles are.*
>
> O. HENRY (1862–1910)
> AMERICAN SHORT STORY WRITER

JULY 4, 1932 . . .

"Time to get up, Son; it's near daylight," said my granddad (whom I called Dad when I stayed with them, which was much of the time). "I've got your breakfast on the table. Better eat a good one—it's gonna be a long day. We've got ham and eggs and hot biscuits, and I made a skillet of red eye gravy."

I had been awake for a long time. The sound of Dad's old coffee mill, grinding his Fox coffee for breakfast, had ended my night's sleep.

Preparation for the big Fourth of July had started days earlier. Yesterday my grandmother killed two chickens. Last night after supper she fried the chicken in her old black skillet until each piece was a golden brown. Since we had no refrigeration, she covered the skillet and left it overnight in the warm oven of her old wood cookstove.

Come morning, the chicken, corn bread, boiled eggs, and apple pie were carefully packed in a basket, along with a fruit jar of water. We could not afford such luxuries as paper plates, so she also packed all other things needed for our picnic dinner. We ate well, though we bought very little at the picnic. I usually had twenty-five cents to spend. Rides on the Ferris wheel or the merry-go-round cost ten cents; a nickel bought a big glass of lemonade.

The trip to the annual Fourth of July picnic in Springdale was one of the year's biggest events for me and my grandparents. That is why I spent the night with them at their home in Spring Valley. My father did not have time for such foolishness.

Let's look at a typical Fourth of July program of events. The following is from *The Springdale News* . . .

JULY 4, 1930

5:00 A.M. . . . . Sunrise Salute
8:30 A.M. . . . . Band Concert on Emma
10:00 A.M. . . . . . . Parade on Emma
10:15 A.M. . . . . Assembly in the Park

America. . . . . . . by Band
Music . . . . Mixed Choir . . . . . . E. E. Guinnup Dir.
Reading. . . . . . . The Declaration of Independence
                 by Wilson Cardwell.
Address . . . . America Yesterday and Today
                 by Grant Smith.
Address . . . . Relation of Highway 71 to N. W.
                 Arkansas by C. F. Burns

Noon
1:00 P.M. . . . . Community Singing
2:00 P.M. . . . . Baseball Game

High School Athletic Field
The Huntsville All Stars
vs
The Fayetteville Arkansas Travellers

4:30 P.M. . . . . Battle Royal in City Park
6:00 P.M. . . . . Band Concert in Park
8:00 P.M. . . . . Fireworks Display

Yesterday, Dad (my grandfather) pumped up all four tires and put three gallons of gas in his old '24 Ford touring car. For youngsters' information, a touring car was a two-seater with a canvas top and side curtains. The curtains were such a bother that they were seldom used, even in the winter.

In order to secure a choice parking space at the picnic grounds (the square block now occupied by our present city administration building), we made sure we were on our way by 6:00 A.M. It was only fifteen miles from Spring Valley to the picnic grounds, but the road was rough, with few places where the Model T could reach speeds of twenty miles per hour. Then, of course, it took quite a long time to pull up the White River hill. A few minutes after 7:00, we pulled into a fine parking space under a large oak tree on the southeast corner of the grounds. Here and there I could see a little activity around the carnival rides and shows, as they prepared for the busy day ahead.

Odors of cooking hamburgers drifted through the park. Even at this hour, some early risers found a hamburger breakfast more appealing than walking downtown to a restaurant.

Picnic activity was in full-swing by 10:00 A.M. Most years, there was a parade down Emma Avenue. Unlike our parades today that are long on horses and trucks, parades then featured brass bands and World War I veterans, dressed in hot woolen uniforms that no longer fit. Floats, usually with a patriotic motif, appeared here and there among marching soldiers.

My most vivid memories of those celebrations are the hundreds of United States flags. The stars and stripes were everywhere—hanging from wires stretched across Emma, from flagpoles in front of every business firm, and even on the radiator caps of cars. A small radiator cap attachment with five small flags was available for about one dollar. Rare indeed was a Model T that did not fly the colors.

MORRIS CLARKSON (October 1993)

A lady named Troutman lived in a little house where the TV cable company office is now located. We lived in a rent house, just west of the Troutman home. As a matter of fact, we rented the house from her. That is the house where I was born. It would be where the TV cable parking lot is now.

Remember the little white house where Fred Owens lived? That house was just west of our house. My granddad Searcy owned that house originally. He also owned the big two-story house on the corner. Granddad sold the houses to a Mr. Loudermilk, and he built a service station and garage in the front yard of the corner house. This station was known as The Bear Cat.

(When I was in high school, the kids referred to this corner garage as The Naked Kitten. Fred Owens operated this from about 1934 until the 1950s—Author.)

Granddad Searcy's house faced west; it was the first house south of The Bear Cat. Directly across Spring Street from my granddad was the two-story brick home of J. J. Banks. Mrs. Troutman's fence on the east of her house was on railroad property, now Commercial Street. As a formality, Frisco sent her a letter, asking her to remove the fence. I'm sure she never removed it, and Frisco didn't really care.

As a very young boy, I looked forward to the annual Fourth of July picnic. I would stand at the front door and watch the Ferris wheel, merry-go-round, and all the concessions. I remember how good the hot dogs and hamburgers smelled. The entire picnic ground was filled with balloons and flags.

I remember the brass band; it was usually one from Fayetteville. Frank Barr was the director. (Probably it was Barr's Boys, according to Roy Nixon, a former member of the band—Author.) *A member of Barr's band later played trombone with John Phillips Sousa. I knew him well; he was one of the finest trombone players I ever heard. He played with us for a number of years and died only recently. His name was Walters. He was known as "Pappy" to all his friends.*

You remember Hila Morgan. Well, her sister had a road show also. Her show played another part of the country. Pappy travelled with that show for years.

The old band shell near the center of the park served as a platform for afternoon speakers. From here politicians, both county and state, made promises—never kept—while painting their opponents as men of morals so low they would not be allowed in the James gang. Well, at least one custom from those days long ago remains with us still.

> *Politics is not a bad profession. If you succeed, there are many rewards. If you disgrace yourself, you can always write a book.*
>
> RONALD REAGAN (B. 1911)
> UNITED STATE PRESIDENT

SUMMER 1923 . . .

A number of cars, mostly Model T Fords, are parked at the Frisco Depot. On the platform, standing in the shade of the new brick structure, people watch as the engineer of a steam locomotive skillfully backs a private coach onto the siding near the Railway Express office. A small crowd, led by a well-dressed portly gentleman, rushes to the observation deck of the private car. He is carrying a large bouquet of flowers.

Through heavily draped coach windows, the crowd gets a glimpse of an attractive sitting room. Electric wall lamps cast a dim glow over the ornate furnishings. Workmen uncouple the small locomotive from the private coach. With a hiss of steam and a puff of black smoke, the switch engine moves back to the main track, hooks on to the remaining cars of the travelling road show, and backs them onto an east siding.

After a well-timed delay, the door of the private coach opens, and a diminutive brunette, her age well concealed by stage makeup, steps to the ornate deck. Smiling, she throws kisses to the crowd.

The portly gentleman steps forward and, reaching upward, hands the bouquet to the smiling lady.

"I'm so happy to be back in your wonderful city," she says. "I enjoy playing here so very, very much. Thank you for this wonderful welcome. The roses are beautiful, just like the people of Springdale. I look forward to seeing each and every one of you at the show tomorrow night."

Hila Morgan had returned again, just as she had for years. As a young high school boy of sixteen, I had the good fortune to attend her last show in Springdale. It was in the summer of 1938. Her large tent was pitched in a vacant lot on West Emma. Sorry, I cannot remember the exact location.

In years previous, the Hila Morgan show tent was erected in the lot between Mill and Spring, north of Johnson Street. It was very near the old swimming pool. I can recall attending her performances when I was so young I sat in Dad's lap and never quite managed to stay awake for the entire show.

Throughout this section of the country, the travelling group of players was better known than most Broadway stars. Miss Morgan's name was a household word. When she was in town, everyone knew and talked about it.

"Hila Morgan is coming next month."

"We're going to see Hila Morgan tonight."

"How about a date to see Hila Morgan?"

I doubt that Lillian Gish or William S. Hart had more fans in Northwest Arkansas. This tiny, ageless lady brought Broadway to Emma and made a few bucks and a lot of friends in the process.

From ad in *The Springdale News,* 1930s:

HILA MORGAN, "herself" and her own Company . . .
One Week in Fayetteville . . . Starts Nov. 3, 1930
NEW PLAYS—NEW VAUDEVILLE—NEW ORCHESTRA
NEW TENT—OLD PRICES—TENT WELL HEATED.

AUGUST 1930 . . .

"Let's go to Springdale Sunday afternoon," I remember Dad saying. "There was a fellow in the store today who said they were having a big celebration at the new airport. It's in that field behind Stobaugh's store. They are supposed to have some stunt flying. Airplanes are coming from all over the country. It oughta be quite a show—and it's free."

For all families of the 1930s, the magic words for any entertainment were "It's free."

Springdale's new airport consisted of one "T" hangar made of galvanized steel. Inside the hangar was Springdale's only airplane, the American Eaglet owned by Bryan Work. Alongside the metal hangar stood a twelve-foot pole with a wind sock on top. A north-south runway, running from Emma on the north to a drainage ditch on the south, was easy to spot; it was the strip recently mowed. The airport was located on East Emma, where the rodeo grounds are today.

Two pilots flying biplanes came from Tulsa, landing early Saturday morning. One, a "stunt pilot," was to take part in the air show Sunday afternoon. The other pilot was here to fly local residents over town in his biplane. By 9:00 A.M., planes from as far as 200 miles away lined each side of the short grass runway. According to *The Springdale News,* so many turned out for the affair Saturday that both pilots were kept busy carrying passengers.

ROBERT "BOB" H. CLARK (OCTOBER 1993)

Before this airport opened, planes used to land in a field up near the Benton County line. I don't remember who owned the field, but it was about a half-mile east of old Highway 71.

One Saturday in 1919, a "barnstormer" landed there. The old World War I plane was piloted by a Captain Johnson.

People in town saw the plane land, and quite a crowd rushed out there. I was fourteen years old and one of the first to arrive. When I found out he was carrying passengers, I rushed back to The Famous Hardware to talk to my dad.

"I sure would like to go up in that plane," I said.

"Son, you don't want to fly in that thing," he answered. "It's probably not safe."

"Oh, yes, I do want to fly," I said. "Dad, I have never been up in a airplane. This is my chance to see Springdale from the air."

Dad thought a few seconds. "Son, how much does this airplane ride cost?"

"Fifteen dollars," I replied. "Fifteen minutes for fifteen dollars."

Well, he gave me the fifteen dollars, and I rushed back to the field.

The pilot put me in the front seat and fastened my belt. He flew from the rear seat. When we were about 2,000 feet high, he cut the engine, tapped me on the shoulder, and asked, "How would you like to do a loop?"

I yelled, "Let 'er go!"

He put the nose down to gain flying speed, then pulled up into two loops in a row. I loved it. I was so enthused when I got home that I wrote an article for

The Springdale News about my flight. I remember one thing from that article. When we were circling town, the afternoon passenger train was pulling out of the Frisco Depot. I described it this way: "The train looked like a giant black snake as it crawled away from the station."

Traffic, according to a news article, was so heavy that extra police were necessary. Cars quickly filled the small space to the west of the runway. Late arrivals parked along both sides of Highway 68.

My most vivid memory of the afternoon was not of the colorful planes or the dashing young men who flew them, but the row of Model T touring cars parked along the west side of the runway. I would estimate that as many as sixty cars were parked side by side. Almost all the cars had their tops raised at a nearly vertical position, blocking off the summer sun while allowing a view of the runway and the sky above.

The highlight of the day was a parachute jump. It was planned that the jumper would land somewhere within the boundaries of the small airfield. Unfortunately, winds were rather high that day. Jumpers then had little control over their descent, so in the interest of safety the jump never occurred.

Bryan (W. J. B.) Work still had his little three-cylinder American Eaglet biplane at this time. Recently I stopped by the Arkansas Air Museum in Fayetteville, and they have one on display.

BOB BOYLE, TULSA, OKLAHOMA (1970)

It must have been in the spring of 1928 or '29. I was a young airplane mechanic just out of school; I was also unemployed. I received a call from a man in Springdale who wanted to know if I would be interested in coming there and doing some work on his airplane. He told me he was in the monument business; he made and sold tombstones for a living. I thought this was most appropriate for a pilot.

I asked him why he didn't just fly it to Tulsa, so I could work on it near my home. He informed me that the plane was not flyable. It was, in fact, disassembled. It seems he had bought the plane after it had returned to earth rather unexpectedly, causing more than a little damage to the stick and canvas construction.

Our conversation was encouraging enough for Bryan Work and me to a arrange a meeting. I needed to look at his American Eaglet and see just what it would take to get it in flying condition.

Fortunately, the Eaglet is about as basic as an airplane can be built and still become airborne. I knew this was a job I could handle.

"Where are we going to work on this plane?" I asked. "We can't pull a complete rebuilding out in the weather."

"I've got that all figured out," answered Bryan. "We've got the old Speas vinegar plant here in town that is not in use. I think I can get that building. It's got a room big enough for the Eaglet, with some left over."

Well, I came to Springdale and took a room by the week. It took the better part of that summer to rebuild the plane. We made it look as good as new. When it was finished, Bryan flew the plane out of the small open field just east of the vinegar works. He was a good pilot. He cleared the power lines by at least twenty feet.

I believe this was the first locally owned plane in Springdale. Bryan did not keep the Eaglet very long. He traded it for a mid-1920s vintage Travelaire biplane.

(Bob Boyle was a top mechanist and mechanic. He operated his own machine shop in Tulsa until his death several years ago—Author.)

> *That strange feeling we had in the war—have you found anything in your lives since to equal it? A sort of splendid carelessness it was, holding us together.*
>
>   NOEL COWARD (1899–1973)
>   BRITISH ACTOR

DECEMBER 7, 1941 . . .

Sunday, December 7, 1941—a dreary, damp day here in Northwest Arkansas. Dark clouds covered the sky. Temperatures were in the low forties. A cold mist— sometimes heavy, sometimes light, other times not at all—descended from the winter sky. Emma Avenue was deserted. It was a day most Springdale citizens chose to stay indoors.

In the kitchen of our home on Emma (third house west of the funeral home) my mother was preparing our usual Sunday pot roast. Dad was not feeling well. "Just a touch of flu, I think," he said. "I'll stay in today; tomorrow I'll be feeling better."

Most Sundays, my parents would have attended services at the First Baptist Church on Holcomb Street. Today, because of the cold damp weather and Dad's flu, they decided to miss Reverend Whittington's sermon.

Since breakfast, Dad had been sitting by the big coal stove reading his Sunday paper. Across the small room, I was looking at the latest *QST Magazine*, daydreaming about ham radio equipment that I could not then afford. Dad lowered the paper. "It sure don't look good over there," he said. Lost in thought, he removed his wire-rimmed glasses and wiped them with his handkerchief. After careful inspection, he put them back on and resumed reading. In the kitchen my mother continued rattling pots and pans.

I was in my third semester of college. I planned to spend the afternoon working on my Physics lab notebook. The morning was mine, and I spent most of it on the radio—visiting with hams in Illinois, Kansas, and Texas.

The old Majestic radio in our living room was tuned to an NBC station featuring a regular Sunday program of Big Band music. I believe, on this particular Sunday, it was the music of Blue Barron and his orchestra. I recall one of the songs they were playing that day: *Dear Mom.* It went like this . . .

> The weather today was cloudy and damp. Your letter arrived, but was missing
> a stamp. Your cake made a hit with the boys here at camp. I love you, dear Mom.

The song was appropriate for this dreary Sunday. Many families had sons and daughters serving in the armed forces or working in defense plants.

We finished our meal, and I returned to my room to work on the Physics assignment. Before starting work on the notebook, I turned on my Breting 9 short wave receiver. I cannot remember whether I was listening to hams on the twenty-meter band or commercial stations on the nineteen-meter band. I do remember, very vividly, hearing a voice full of fear and excitement, repeating over and over: "We are under attack . . . we are under attack . . . we are under attack." The operator described the scene of destruction, the bombing, the large number of planes overhead, and the general horror of Pearl Harbor.

I had no idea where Pearl Harbor was; at that time I had never heard of it. Rushing into our living room, I tuned back and forth across the broadcast band on the Majestic. There was no mention of Pearl Harbor or any attack by enemy planes. I told Dad and Mother what I had just heard. Dad never had much patience with ham radio or ham operators. To him it was something on which kids wasted time and money. Dad had positive opinions about hobbies: if you enjoyed something, it was too expensive and, in all probability, sinful as well.

"It's just some of those kids playing with their radio," he said. "There's nothing to it. Don't you think it's time you get to work on your studies?"

He had hardly finished his sentence when all hell broke loose on the broadcast radio. Every station had news of the attack, most of it inaccurate. Every few minutes you would hear an announcement: "All military personnel, return to base immediately. All military personnel, return to base immediately."

Within the next few minutes, news began to come through in more detail. I put on my raincoat and cap and walked down town. I wanted to see what others thought of the news. The only place in town that was open was Arthur Dyes' newsstand (#78). He was alone in the shop.

Mr. Dyes was a small gentleman, who often carried an umbrella. I thought he bore a striking resemblance to Neville Chamberlain. I had a lot of respect for him and his opinions. I told him the news; he had heard nothing about it. He assured me that it was of little importance, nothing to be excited about. "The United States could lick those Japs in two weeks," he said. "They wouldn't dare attack us."

He was not alone in this opinion. Some news people on the radio were saying much the same thing.

> *The belief in the possibility of a short decisive war appears to be one of the most ancient and dangerous of human illusions.*
>
> ROBERT LYND (1879–1949)

The following morning about 6:00 A.M., I left for the university campus. Normally, few professors or students were up and about at such an early hour. Today it was different. Most University of Arkansas students were deeply concerned. Many had stayed up all night listening to the news. Classes that morning were involved with an analysis of the situation in the Pacific and the impact a war there would have on the United States.

Perhaps my English professor, a young Rhodes Scholar, summed up the Pearl Harbor attack better than anyone. After showing us maps of the Pacific and explaining distances involved; fighting conditions we would likely encounter; the estimated size of the Japanese Navy, Army, and Air Force; and the merits of the Japanese Zero compared to the Curtis P40, he said:

"To say I'm alarmed is an understatement. I'm scared shitless."

Near noon, Dick Cantrell, Kathryn Brogdon, LeRoy "Brushwood" Nelson, and I walked down town for lunch at the Blue Mill. After eating, we walked up to the square. A crowd of people, engaged in animated conversation, was gathered on the southeast corner in front of Guisinger's Music House.

"What's going on?" I asked one of the group.

"The president is going to make an announcement in a few minutes," he replied. "Everyone thinks he is going to declare war."

Guisinger's had a large loudspeaker tied directly over their front entrance. Wires led from the speaker to a radio inside the music store. Within minutes we heard President Roosevelt's voice. Few there will ever forget those words—"the cowardly and dastardly attack" . . . "a date which will live in infamy" . . . "a state of war has existed. . . ." President Roosevelt spoke slowly and deliberately. Everyone fully realized when he finished speaking before Congress that each and every one of us were at war. We also knew that we must win the war with Japan and Germany at any cost. Now we knew: no more guessing, no more waiting, no more talk of defense. That one speech signaled a change affecting the lives of everyone in America. Our generation would never be the same.

Trips to the Frisco Depot became a nightly ritual for many of Springdale's citizens. The nine o'clock passenger train became longer and longer, as more troops were moved by rail. During the five-minute stop people visited with the soldiers on board, often giving them food, cigarettes, or sometimes postcards of the area to send home.

As I watched each departing train, I realized that my time was coming very soon.

When I enlisted in the Air Force, I left town on the Frisco. Three years and a few months later, I returned the same way.

CHAPTER 2

Returning Home

*God gave us our memories so that we might have roses in
December.*

J. M. BARRIE (1860–1937)
BRITISH PLAYWRIGHT

Dad looked at the luminous hands of the alarm clock on the bedside table; it
was almost 4:00 A.M. The small bedroom was hot and still. Quite often at this
time of year a welcome summer breeze blowing through the south window
brought relief from the heat, but not tonight. He relinquished all thoughts of sleep.

My mother, aware that he had spent a sleepless night, lowered her feet to the floor,
saying, "I'm wide awake; why don't we get up? I'll make us a pot of coffee. We should
leave before five. The train might be a few minutes early."

"That's fine with me," replied Dad. "I have been awake since two-thirty."

Dad backed his old '32 Plymouth coupe from the driveway at 615 Allen, slowly
drove along Allen and Holcomb, then east on Emma to the Frisco Depot. Here and
there, a lighted window in one of the small homes cast a feeble beam of light across a
grassy lawn. Pollution and progress had not yet come to Springdale. The air, still and
quiet, was heavy with the sweet smell of summer.

Parking near the depot, Dad mentioned that they appeared to be the first to arrive.
Soon other cars would join them, waiting for the early train. By the soft yellow glow
from lights along the dock, plus the light above "Springdale" on the depot, they could
see the green Railway Express truck parked behind the express office. Beyond the
semaphore, this side of the express office, was an unused, locked, dark green door. A
sign above the door read "Colored Waiting Room."

In my months working for Western Union, I never knew of a "colored" person to
use the room. An inside door of the little room opened into the Frisco office. Though
unused, the room was kept clean, as if expecting a passenger.

"Civil rights" was a term as yet unfamiliar to us. One of our better restaurants, in
1950, had a short history of the city on the back of its menu. The menu proudly proclaimed: "Springdale is a city of 1,800 citizens—all white."

On the red brick wall, left of the "colored" waiting room door, was the "colored" drinking fountain, thoughtfully placed there by the Frisco tracks. "White" passengers were provided with a duplicate water fountain placed to the right of the other waiting room door.

All was quiet—the only sound breaking the morning silence was the chirping of birds in the trees in the vacant lot behind Late Chevrolet announcing the imminent approach of dawn. The rattle of express cart wheels on the old brick walkway, extending from Emma Avenue northward past the Railway Express Agency office, told them Paul Jones was opening the express office.

As I stepped from the train that September morning in 1945, old memories came rushing up Emma Avenue like winds before a storm, blotting out the present: Saturday night dates—taking my girl to the movies at the Concord—cokes after school at Penrod's—parades down Emma—Fourth of July picnics in the city park (one block north of where I was now standing)—and my very unpleasant memory of delivering groceries for Wink Needham's Corner Grocery. While in the Air Force, when things seemed really bad, I thought back to delivering groceries; suddenly my problems became much smaller.

The Corner Grocery occupied a choice business location in the 1930s. The southeast corner of Emma and Holcomb, two doors east of The Famous Hardware, directly across the street from Lichlyter's, was one of the best locations on Emma. The old brick building dated back to the 1880s. Springdale Hardware, a number of grocery stores, doctors' offices, beauty shops, and, for a time, the post office had been housed in this structure.

"Wink" (Winifred) Needham, his wife Georgia, and Georgia's sister, Ann McDonald, ran the store. Noted for their excellent home delivery service, the store employed a full-time delivery boy. On Saturdays, business was so heavy they pulled the full-time employee inside to wait on customers and hired a high school boy to do deliveries. For a few unpleasant months, I was the Saturday delivery boy.

Wink was rather short and heavy-set, and his face looked younger than his sixty years. A small piece of sandy-colored hair seemed to constantly dangle in front of his gold-rimmed glasses. Mr. Needham was scrupulously honest and was one of the nicest people I ever worked for.

I remember repairing a Zenith radio for Mr. Needham back in my high school days. At the time I thought their home was one of the most attractive in Springdale. Fifty-five years later, I still think so. The Needham place at 408 South Shiloh is now the home of Mr. and Mrs. Harry L. Blundell. The next time you drive by, take a look at one of the prettiest trees in Northwest Arkansas. It is in front of their house, out near the sidewalk.

"Dressed" chickens were one of our big Saturday sellers. Our work day began at 6:30 A.M. My first chore on Saturday was to pick up three dozen live chickens at a produce across the tracks. As soon as I unloaded the coops, Ann and Georgia started to work in the back room wringing chicken necks. The room became a bloody mess within minutes.

While Georgia and Ann killed chickens, I carried bucket after bucket of scalding hot water to the back room and poured it in clean washtubs placed on the floor. For the next hour chicken feathers flew so fast that it looked like a snow storm in the foul (no pun intended) smelling room.

Chicken innards were thrown in cardboard boxes. A few layers of newspapers in the bottom kept the carton from becoming soggy. By 9:00 A.M. the "dressed" chickens were in the walk-in Koch refrigerated cooler. Mr. Needham was very proud of his meat department. The walk-in freezer not only served a vital purpose, but added a touch of class to his immaculately clean butcher shop. Recently purchased, it was one of the few such coolers in Springdale.

To Mr. Needham's constant embarrassment, Mrs. Needham (Georgia) had trouble with the name. I can still see his red face when Georgia would yell across the crowded store, "Wink, reach in the crotch and hand me a plump chicken for Mrs. Smith." The next time Georgia walked by him, he would whisper, "It's KOCH, Georgia, dammit— KOCH." Mrs. Needham was too busy to listen.

By 10:00 A.M. the store received enough telephone orders to fill several metal grocery baskets. As each order was filled, the metal baskets were placed in a row on the floor in the storeroom. I was supposed to deliver them in order. However, Mrs. Needham promised any customer calling that her order would be next. By 10:30, all semblance of order was down the tube. Now, it was management by crisis; order of delivery was dictated by the last phone call.

My orders were: go to the back door; step inside the kitchen or sometimes an enclosed back porch; put the groceries on a table the customer had cleared in advance; and put all perishables in the ice box. Sounds simple enough . . .

Of course, I had my problems. For example, one of our better customers was always in a hurry, needing the groceries "right away." I would rush to the house on Maple Avenue, only to find the door locked, and no one home. When I returned to the store, Mrs. __________ would be on the phone wanting to know when we were going to deliver her groceries. It seemed she had "only stepped out for a minute," and, of course, that was the minute I arrived. We understood and no one became upset, but it usually took two or more trips to get her groceries delivered. Then, of course, there were Guy Howard's dogs. With fangs bared and bristles raised, they dared me to come one step closer to the cleared table. All the while, Miss Eva Howard (Guy's sister) assured me they "wouldn't bite a biscuit." I was not really interested in their eating habits. I just wanted out of the kitchen with as little bloodshed as possible.

In snowy or rainy weather I was soaking wet by noon and at least two hours behind

with my deliveries. I would grab a dry shirt, eat as quickly as possible, and return to
the old 1933 Dodge delivery truck. Normally, it was well after dark before I made my
last delivery. We closed at 9:00 P.M. While waiting for closing time, my job was to clean
up the chicken room. After closing, we cleaned the vegetable counter, put all the unsold
fresh vegetables in the cooler, and swept the store. I had one more job before I would
be paid for the day's work. I had to load the chicken guts in the truck, drive to a farm
west of Springdale, dump the mess in some pig pens Mr. Needham owned, and then
return to the store. The day ended around 10:15 P.M. Mr. Needham paid me my wages
for the fifteen hour day at ten cents a hour. He counted out to me $1.50 in cash.

If Joyce's was still open, and it usually was, I would treat myself to a nickel root
beer. They served it in large stainless steel mugs which were kept in the freezer. I remember how I enjoyed drinking from those frost-covered metal mugs.

Speaking of Joyce's, they had a bench along the east wall, directly in front of the
tobacco counter. Roy Joyce, the owner, liked to sit there, look out the window, and
visit with friends. He usually had a few of the Emma Avenue crowd as company. One
day several of the fellows were visiting and looking across the street at The Famous
Hardware. During a lull in conversation, Roy said, "Fellows, I want you to look real
careful. You are looking at the only automatic store in Springdale. That store (The
Famous) literally runs itself."

ROBERT "BOB" H. CLARK

*My dad and Ed Cummings were raised near Hindsville. The old home place
is three miles due east of Hindsville. I am not sure where Ed Cummings lived,
but Dad and Ed were good friends from their youth.*

*When they got old enough, they were kicked out of the family nest. There
were thirteen in Dad's family—ten boys and three girls. A 460-acre farm just
won't support that many adults.*

*Dad and Ed opened a little drug store in Hindsville. After a year or so it became
apparent that the store was not doing enough business to continue operation.*

*The Cherokee Strip was opening up over in the Indian Nation, so they headed
in that direction. They came to Grove, Oklahoma, and decided it looked promis-
ing. They opened a drug store there.*

*It was not very profitable, and after a year or so, when it burned down, they
decided to go a little farther west. They got on their horses and rode to Tulsa.
This was in 1906 or '07. Tulsa was a frontier town of about 1,500 people.*

*It was a rainy, dreary day when the two tired young men arrived at their
destination.*

*They came to a muddy crossroads and, remaining in their saddles, surveyed
the town. Mud was more than ankle-deep. Board sidewalks, in front of a few
shabby, frame business houses were filled with Indians, rough-looking cow hands,
and more than a few drunks.*

*Ed turned in his saddle and looked at Dad. "Bob, what do you think about
this place?" he asked.*

Dad replied, "Ed, this town is never going to amount to a damn."

Ed was quick to agree. They turned on their horses and headed back for Northwest Arkansas.

A few years later, one of Tulsa's largest oil fields was located near the spot where they had appraised the town.

Ed and Bob returned to Springdale. In 1907, they purchased the W. T. Farrar Merchandise Company, located on the corner of Emma and Mill (#65). The Farrar store sold a wide variety of merchandise, including clothing, furniture, Queen's Ware, dry goods, hardware, and coffins. The store actually catered to the women's trade more than it did to the men's.

The name of the store was changed to The Famous Hardware. Ed and Dad decided to dispose of all merchandise except hardware. Of course, coffins and coffin hardware were considered a part of any well-stocked hardware. It was especially appropriate for The Famous. Down the street, this side of the S. R. Wilson Company, was Springdale's undertaking parlor. It was run by Joe Nix. Joe and Dad were good friends.

By golly, the new store took off. From the beginning it was a profitable venture and soon became one of Springdale's best-known stores.

Dad was a pipe smoker. I have no idea how many pipes he had. He kept them placed all over the store, usually on a shelf with the bowl supported by a corner. No matter where he was in the store, he always had a pipe within reach. Sometimes a customer would "test" him.

"Where is your pipe, Bob?" they would ask.

To the customer's amusement, Dad would take a few steps to the right or to the left, reach to a shelf, and pull out a pipe.

In 1934, The Famous moved to its last location on Emma (#48-south side, third building west of Holcomb).

Waiting for the arrival of the southbound Frisco passenger train in the pre-dawn darkness, my parents must have expected, and were certainly entitled to, more from their returning son than a preoccupied greeting.

I looked through the first light of dawn at the outline of Jeff Brown's Feed Mill. It was still the same old sheet-iron building. I had hoped that it would at least have a coat of paint by now.

Turning my gaze to the rear of the train, I could see Paul Jones, his revolver strapped to his side, busy unloading a Railway Express car. I wanted to walk up to his office and see if Blackie, his old German Shepherd, was still alive. I remembered how, when I was working for Western Union in 1939, Blackie would wait for me every morning at the corner of the Late Chevrolet showroom. I would scratch his head between his ears, then we would run to the depot together.

The old semaphore was still there. In August of 1939 I took the job of climbing the thirty foot ladder every day to replace the empty kerosene lantern with a full one. For this small effort they paid two dollars a month. It seemed like a good deal—until winter came, and the metal ladder became covered with ice. After a couple of trips up the icy ladder I resigned my position. I was surprised to see it was still not electrified.

Many mornings before the war, when I was expecting an express shipment, I would give up two hours sleep and meet the morning train. I often ordered radio gear from Bob Henry Radio in Butler, Missouri. By arising at 4:00 A.M. and waiting at the express office, I could get my package a few hours sooner; such is the impatience of youth.

I looked into the dark northern sky. Was it only five years ago that Frank Cunningham, a Frisco employee, had taught me how to build and fly those large box kites? We launched our kites from the railway platform in front of the office. Frank had to stay nearby, listening for the telegraph sounder. Fort Smith often called Springdale. I can still hear the sounder clattering away . . . ND FS . . . ND FS . . . ND FS . . . Frank would have to run and answer the call. (ND was the call for Springdale; FS, for Fort Smith).

Most of the time we could get our kite in the air before being bothered with mundane affairs, like Frisco railroad business. We never lost a kite to the many telegraph lines so near our launching site. No doubt about it—Frank knew his kite building. Often we could tie the line to the semaphore tower; a large box kite would stay up for hours.

I can see the station agent in my mind's eye, hunched over his ancient Vibroplex "bug," sending and receiving railroad dispatch messages. In its polished oak holder over his desk, the telegraph sounder clattered away. To make the intermittent clicks louder, he kept a Prince Albert tobacco can wedged between the sounder and its oak holder. This amplified the sound, enabling him to copy code from almost anywhere in the building. Isaac Newton "Newt" Harris was a small man. Neatly dressed in a white shirt and worn black vest, he wore the traditional dark green visor popular with turn of the century telegraphers. His dark eyes, set in a serious, unsmiling face, peered through small gold-rimmed glasses.

It was said that he could pause while copying a message, go to the customer window, sell a ticket, make change, return to his old typewriter, and resume copying the message without missing a word. I am sure the story is true.

The Western Union office remained unchanged from my years there. Occupying the southwest corner of the Frisco waiting room, the telegraph area was defined from the rest of the waiting room by waist-high desks on the east and north. Frances Turner was the Western Union agent from the early 1930s until after the war. A lady of endless patience, she probably wanted to kill me on more than one occasion. I was a trainee for a few months, which meant that I ran errands, delivered telegrams, kept the old coal stove going, tried to master touch-typing on the telegraph printer, and learned the Morse Code.

A regulator clock hung on the brick wall by the front door. Daily, at 11:00 A.M., the watch would be re-set by telegraph line. Everyone assumed it was the correct time— this was high tech for the 1930s and '40s.

Every morning without fail, Mr. Kennan (father of A. J. Kennan) walked from his shop to the depot to set his watch. He would arrive about five minutes before eleven. Standing in front of the regulator, his large pocket watch in hand, he waited for the "click," signifying re-set. When the large clock hands snapped to 11:00, he would punch in the stem of his watch, setting it exactly with the latest Railroad Time.

Mr. Kennan's watch repair shop was located between Penrod's and the Palace Barber shop. He was an excellent watch repairman. For a brief time after World War I, he ventured into the phonograph and record business. I remember going into his store with my mother, probably about 1925. She was a Jimmy Rogers fan and bought all his new records.

Extremely hard of hearing, Mr. Kennan was killed when he drove in front of a Frisco train at the Emma Avenue crossing. Though the engineer keep blowing the train whistle, Mr. Kennan never stopped; in all probability he was unaware of the approaching train.

The clattering sound of express wagons on the rough brick platform interrupted my memories. I turned my attention to my parents. After a rather awkward greeting, I loaded my gear in the trunk of the car. The three of us squeezed into the small seat and then drove home. They had purchased the home while I was in Europe. When I entered the Air Force, they lived in a house owned by Mrs. Sharp (grandmother of Thelma and Wilma Webb) at 404 Emma Street, one block west of the beautiful old Deaver home.

Emma Avenue was named after Emma Dupree Deaver, wife of Jacob P. Deaver. They were the early residents of the Deaver house. Mr. and Mrs. Frank Deaver and their children (Kennedy, Bill, and Sarah) lived there when I moved to Springdale in 1938.

The date was September 9. After a lot of talk and a good breakfast, I took a hot bath. I was now a civilian. (I found this a strange, and somewhat disturbing, thought.) My civilian clothes no longer fit. I weighed 165 pounds, some 36 pounds more than I did when I last wore them. Anyway, I felt almost naked. I was reluctant to venture out in such clothing. During my years in the Air Force, the term "civilian" was used with unconcealed contempt. Something like this . . ."He's nothing but a G__ d___ featherbedding civilian." I knew my uniform must go, but for today I wanted to keep it on.

A trip to Wilson's and Lichlyter's that afternoon took most of my three hundred bucks mustering-out pay. I overcame my uncomfortable feeling of wearing "civvies" very quickly. After this day, the only time I wore my uniform was when I served on the American Legion Honor Guard for funerals of returning servicemen. Within a few years, an expanding waist line made wearing my old uniform a near impossibility. I donated it to the Shiloh Museum.

Suddenly it dawned on me that there was going to be no rest—no so-called period of readjustment to civilian life. There was simply too much to be done.

I wanted to return to school and certainly had no wish to waste an entire semester. I was in the registrar's office at the University of Arkansas less than forty-eight hours after

I arrived home. School had been in session for almost ten days. They agreed to let me register, but warned that I would be in for a rough time. A large, and for the most part unexpected, influx of veterans filled classes to overflowing. Books for required courses were unavailable. While most professors were anxious to extend every courtesy, and far too much latitude, to returning veterans, other professors maintained a less patriotic posture.

Now that I was enrolled in school, I needed transportation. I rolled out my '37 Harley Davidson and went to work on it. I had removed the battery before leaving for the service. Lifting it from a shelf, I added distilled water and tried charging it. Nothing doing—it was dead. I was not surprised; it was not very good when I left. Both tires were flat and needed replacing. Before leaving, I had instructed my dad to remove the spark plugs, squirt a little oil in each cylinder, and kick the motor over, at least once a month. This paid off. I filled the gas tank, checked the oil, jumped the battery, and, with a couple of kicks, the motor came to life. Within hours the machine was ready to ride.

For many years, Silas Graham owned a blacksmith shop on Mill Street. The old wooden building was located on the east side of Mill, south of Johnson Street.

Sil was well known for his eccentric habits and lack of patience. Posted in the blacksmith shop was a large hand-lettered sign. It read: "BOYS KEEP OUT." The sign was a result of a lot of boys wanting him to repair their bicycles, usually for nothing.

Silas found it difficult to say more than four words without throwing in a few colorful cuss words.

One of his favorite lines was, "Wa, Wa, by G__, whatja bring it to me fer?" Even though he knew he could, and would, do the work brought to him, the conversation usually started with that line.

I remember when I first bought my motorcycle from Gail Brown. I needed two small brackets to hold the front light. I went to Sil. I had a drawing showing a simple right-angle bracket made from a four-inch piece of strap iron. All he needed to do was saw off four inches of strap, fasten it in a vise, and bend it at 90 degrees.

After the "Wa, Wa, by G__, whatja bring it to me fer?," I explained my needs.

He looked at me with a unsmiling face. "I don't know anything about motor sickles," he snapped.

I patiently explained that he did not need to know anything about motorcycles. I picked up a scrap of cardboard and bent it into the shape I needed. "Just bend a piece of strap iron into this shape," I pleaded.

"Wa, Wa, iff'n yore so G__ d___ smart, go do it yourself," he growled.

Then he took the paper from my hand, looked at it a moment, and made two of the prettiest brackets you could ask for.

"How much do I owe you, Sil?" I asked.

"Oh, I guess it ought to be worth a quarter," he replied. "I charge a little more for working on motor sickles."

I found my four years absence from college had changed my entire attitude. Somehow, I could not get serious about school. I had one teacher I liked very much. A West Point graduate who had left the diplomatic corps because he was anything but diplomatic, Professor Hamilton taught American History. I looked forward to every class.

Including myself, there were three veterans in his history class. When he called the roll each morning, we would answer with a "Here, sir" loud enough to jangle the nerves of the early morning customers of George's, who, being "hung over," were trying the old "hair of the dog" cure for their throbbing heads.

Speaking of George's, it was here that I tried my first pickled pig's foot. I might mention it was also my last taste of that Southern delicacy. The old cafe occupies a hallowed place in the minds of thousands of U. of A. students. George's Majestic Cafe (now Lounge) is a most unique establishment with a long and interesting history. Many of the students of fifty years ago have fond memories of sitting in the little beer garden behind the dingy cafe, holding hands with a date, and spending their entire week's allowance on beer. Overhead, a summer moon shining brightly in an unpolluted sky cast its yellow light through unkempt scraggly vines. Only youth can be so easily and cheaply transported from reality—transforming a dismal little area, within feet of the Frisco tracks, into a romantic rendezvous. Ah, to be young again!

Three years away from school had changed my priorities. A degree in Physics had lost much of its appeal. I wanted to stay right here in Springdale. I decided to quit college.

> *It was always thus, impelled by a state of mind which is destined not to last, that we make our irrevocable decisions.*
>
> MARCEL PROUST (1871–1922)
> FRENCH NOVELIST

I soon realized that my motorcycle, while great fun to ride, was really not a practical means of transportation. A fellow student offered me five hundred dollars for it. I sold out. I was without a motorcycle for the next two years.

Dad wanted to give me a car when I came home from the Air Force. New cars were, for all practical purposes, unavailable. He bought a nice 1941 Chevrolet, a pretty sky-blue Fleetline. I think both he and my mother were glad to see the motorcycle go.

So . . . here I was: February 1946, twenty-four years old, no degree, no job, with a grand total of seven hundred dollars in the bank.

Well, it really was not so bad. I had been thinking of my options all during the war. Perhaps the real reason I quit school was that the salary offered to those graduating with a B. S. in Physics back in '46 was rather low. As I remember, a starting salary of $2,400 per year was about average. For this small sum, you had to move to one of the larger cities, most of which seemed to be on the East Coast. I could earn about the same amount doing any number of jobs in Springdale and would not have to live in the Northeast. I have always believed that the only reason anyone would live north of the Mason-Dixon line is because he could not get work in the South. Even this is not reason enough to get me to live in Washington, D. C. or New York City.

Late Chevrolet was still located on Emma, immediately west of the tracks. John Late, the owner, started his business in Johnson, Arkansas, around the turn of the century. He purchased a wagon and team and earned a living hauling lime from the kiln. He soon expanded to hauling other cartage. When the "new fangled" horseless carriages started becoming popular, Mr. Late decided to go into the new business and became a Chevrolet dealer. Now well past retirement age and in failing health, his temper was something to behold. His customers traded with him because they liked his product, not Mr. Late. They tried to avoid the ill-tempered old man when possible. Let me say here, he was badly misunderstood. John Late was always more than fair in any dealings with me, and his gruff exterior could be penetrated, very easily, with a little understanding.

REUBEN BRYANT (September 1993)

The street just east of the Pioneer Lumber Company and Late Chevrolet used to be called Railroad Street. A few years ago it was renamed Commercial Street. The reason they called it Railroad was because it was railroad property.

John Late's property on the corner of Emma and Railroad just came to the east edge of the sidewalk, along the east side of his building. John used Frisco property for his car lot. He kept all his used cars backed up against the railroad dock. New cars were parked along the sidewalk.

Shorty Smith—you remember him—lived just on the right after you crossed the White River Bridge; he was White River Red's right-hand man. Well, Shorty went up there one day and parked his car by the Frisco dock. John watched Shorty park, then came charging out of his office.

"If you don't move that car, I'll have it towed away," said John. "You are on my parking lot. I'll have my wrecker move it."

"When you do," replied Shorty, "you better have me a new car sitting in its place. You don't own any of this property; it all belongs to Frisco. You are the one parking in the wrong place."

John raised up on his good leg and waved his cane. "I do own this; Frisco don't have a thing to do with it."

"If I was you," answered Shorty, "I would go in the depot and check with them, just to be sure you are not on their property."

After Shorty left town, John walked to the depot and asked if they knew where the Frisco property line ended.

"Our property line extends to the east side of the sidewalk," they told John. He never threatened anyone again, but he continued parking his cars on Frisco property.

If I remember correctly, Frisco owned ninety feet on each side of the tracks. They had a 180-foot right of way. Many of the houses on the east side of Holcomb, especially up near the crossing, were using Frisco property for a back yard. The problem may have been corrected by now.

During this period in 1946 Dad was working for Late Chevrolet as shop foreman. I might add that Mr. Late and my dad had a stormy relationship. Dad would work for him three months or so, then get mad and quit. They would shout at each other to the amusement of other employees within earshot of the confrontation. Though there was threatening talk, they never came to blows. Dad would then go to work as a barber at the Palace. Some time later, after these temper tantrums between two equally unreasonable adults, Mr. Late would start driving slowly past our house—several times a day—until he finally found Dad in the yard or garden. (Dad would be watching from a window, waiting for the old man to drive by once or twice before he would find a "chore" to do outside.) Mr. Late would stop, sound his horn, and motion for Dad to come and get in the car. (John Late was very overweight and had a bad leg, making walking difficult.)

They would talk for twenty minutes or so; then Dad would exit the car with a solemn look on his face. Entering the house, he would smile and say, "Well, I'm going back to work for John. You know, he really is a pretty nice old man to work for. Besides, he gave me a two dollar raise."

Less than one week after I quit school, I dropped by Late Chevrolet. John was sitting behind his worn oak desk near the east showroom window. He lifted his bad leg up onto the desk top, glared at me for a few seconds, leaned back in the old oak office chair, and said, "Your dad says you quit school. What'cha plannin' on doin' now?"

"Well, I don't really know just yet," I replied. "I am thinking about putting in a radio shop. I'm a pretty fair repairman."

"Yep, I remember you workin' for Coy Cantrell down the street before you went to the war. I think you could do good if you put your head to it and worked," answered Mr. Late. "I'll make you a proposition—you can have the building next door, the one between my showroom and the Ritz Cafe, free of charge. All you've got to do is install a few radios in new cars as they come in. There won't be many for a good while, as we only get a load now and then. When we start gettin' a lot of 'em, we can work out other arrangements. I want to be fair with you."

"Let me think it over," I replied. "I'll give you my answer in a couple of days. By the way, I really appreciate your offer."

He never answered. Without smiling, he lifted up his walking stick and waved me aside.

CHAPTER 3

Bruce's Electric Shop

*The best career advice to give to the young is "Find out what
you like doing best and get someone to pay you for doing it."*

KATHERINE WHITEHORN (B. 1926)
BRITISH JOURNALIST

When confronted with a problem, I first list my options, then choose the least unpleasant, in lieu of the best or most logical solution. It seemed I now had three choices: return to school; go to work for someone—if I could get a job; or go into business for myself.

The G. I. Bill would pay for my education, a factor making choice number one well worth consideration. Choice number two was eliminated immediately. I did not have enough training to command a respectable salary from any employer I could think of. I took inventory of my qualifications for operating a business, my third and last choice. This choice appeared equally unfavorable.

I knew nothing about bookkeeping or merchandising. My lack of experience was rivaled only by my lack of business acumen. Even more discouraging was my financial situation. My bank account was down to slightly less than seven hundred dollars.

My only skill seemed to be electronics, and 99% of my knowledge there was with two-way communications equipment, mostly aircraft radio—not the type of equipment I would likely encounter if I opened a radio shop.

With the confidence born of ignorance and youth, I decided to go into business for myself. In less than twenty-four hours, I made a decision on how I would spend the balance of my life.

Granddad Vaughan gave me some advice when I was ten years old. He said, "Son, when faced with a problem, go with your first idea. The longer you think about it, the more likely you are to make a mistake. Most of the time your first idea is the course you really like best—that is why you thought of it first. You will always be better off doing what you like best."

My affirmative answer to Mr. Late was delivered early the following morning. My shop would be in what he called the "Case Room." Some years before, he had added the Case line of farm equipment to his business, Mr. Late bought the building immediately west of his auto dealership. After remodeling, the building included a showroom, a parts room, and an office for J. I. Case tractors and farm implements. Several people reminded me that my shop was located in the old Cozy Cafe building.

For some unknown reason Mr. Late dropped the idea before stocking the building. He did sell a few tractors, but soon became disenchanted with the tractor business and padlocked the empty Case Room. This was the building he offered me.

It was ideal. The light green paint of the large showroom looked like new. I had a glassed-in office at the rear of the room, adequate electrical outlets, two nice show-windows in front, plus an enclosed heated garage in the back. The garage was perfect for auto radio repair and installation. It was all anyone could wish for. I could not have designed a better building for my use.

CLIFFORD SAMUEL (September 1993)

In 1940, when I first moved to Springdale to work for Coger, I had a room upstairs at Mr. Little's house. The house was next to the old church building, up towards The Bear Cat.

I don't remember how much I paid for rent; I think it was two dollars a week. Anyway, I took two meals a day at the Cozy restaurant—breakfast and supper. I paid by the week—three dollars for twelve meals. They were closed on Sunday.

One day after supper, "Buckshot" (Mr. Smith) called me off to one side. "Clifford," he said, "I really hate to do this. I wish I could get by without mentioning it, but I have to raise your weekly bill. I have tried to figure a way around it, but starting next week I'm going to have to charge you a quarter more a week. For $3.25 I can make a little money. As it is, I'm just not making it."

That doesn't sound like much money, but I was making only ten dollars a week. Over half of my salary was going for room and board.

Now, half a century later, I often look backward to those years. In retrospect, I am sure the term "Golden Years" should apply not to old age—the end of life—but to the twenties and thirties. This is the golden time of one's life. The tedious years of childhood are left behind, and all that is fine and good is yet to be experienced. Marriage, starting a business, your first child, raising a family—these are the "Golden Years." This was especially true for young men and women returning from World War II. The long promised "post-war years" were ours—ours to do with as we pleased. We had earned them. They were paid for with hard work, discomfort beyond comprehension, boredom, stark terror, and blood. Thousands of our generation would never experience adulthood. Some were buried in some distant land or at sea, while others just disappeared, erased from this planet in a split second of unbelievable horror by the Gods of War.

The twenties is a time of life when you have the enthusiasm and energy to correct your mistakes, to recover from almost any illness, and to overcome those troublesome obstacles that seem to occur inevitably just as success or happiness is within reach. The road ahead appears to be straight and smooth. Though we know there will be bumps along the way, we choose not to think of them, confident that when they appear, we will steer our way safely around them, uninterrupted on our way through the happy life ahead.

In 1946, by most standards, I made a poor choice. I exchanged a college education for the life of a tradesman. After all, radio repairmen were more or less on the bottom of the social and economic ladder. We were ranked with shoe repairmen, auto mechanics, plumbers, carpenters, painters, and others who earn their living by producing and maintaining consumer products. I did not mind what others thought. I have always believed there is dignity in creating and producing useful goods and services, though the wages may be modest. Social parasites, and there are many, often earn a fortune producing absolutely nothing. They receive so little satisfaction from life.

Though I did not realize it at the time, I was among the fortunate few who would witness, at very close range, the death of radio, the coming of television, and the invention of the transistor. In 1945, tape recorders, LP records, pocket radios, stereo, video recorders, and computers were only daydreams in the minds of a few inventors and scientists. Few today realize the social and economic changes wrought by the explosion of technology in electronics. The experience alone was worth more—far more—than gold.

The Pioneer Lumber Company, a Springdale institution for many years, was located directly across the street from my shop. It was owned and operated by the Deaver family. The large dark red building extended from the old Concord Theater, east to Railroad Street, now named Commercial Street.

A noticeable feature of the old building was the Sherwin-Williams Paint trademark prominently displayed to the right of the front doors—a globe of the earth, painted in white, red, and yellow. Above the globe, a paint bucket, tilted at a sharp angle, poured red paint on the north pole from where it ran in all directions. The lettering stated proudly: SHERWIN-WILLIAMS . . . We Cover The Earth.

Dimension lumber was stored in the east shed. The Pioneer business office, paint store, and small hardware department occupied the center building. Between the office and the Concord Theater were two small rooms where glass, doors, and windows were stored. At one time these rooms served as a cabinet shop, but that part of the company moved to a new building south of the offices in 1946. Through dingy upstairs windows above the office, you could make out forms of boxes and clutter unmoved for years.

Sliding doors on each end of the lumber shed were open from 7:00 A.M. until 6:00 P.M. Customers could drive their trucks through the north or Emma Avenue door, pick up a load of lumber, and depart through the south door.

On our hottest days a nice breeze blew through the structure, sweeping out hot air accumulated under the high roof. This cool, shady old building was a favorite rendezvous for the town "winos," and there were many. What could be more ideal? The liquor store was directly across the street. To the west of the liquor store was the Blue Castle beer joint; a few doors east was the old Concord Tavern.

Every few minutes you could see one of the red-faced fraternity make his unsteady way to the liquor store. Within minutes he would return to the lumber shed, a pint of cheap grape wine in a back pocket of his overalls.

When one needed a drink to keep the glow going, he simply ducked behind one of the stacks of lumber. When nature called, they were a little more discreet, walking to the south end of the shed where they used a dark corner. I am sure more than one tear was shed when, in the early 1950s, Clark and Deaver Hardware merged with the Pioneer Lumber Company, tore the old building down, and replaced it with one of Emma's most attractive business structures. Another Springdale landmark disappeared into history.

In 1936, we had a store on the Huntsville Square. Located east of the old court house, the building served as our living quarters and for whatever business Dad was trying that particular week. My dad and mother had a barber and beauty shop in the west half of the building. The east half of the structure served for Dad's "get rich quick" attempts. Business ventures that he tried included a dress shop, a grocery store, and a public bath house—but not the kind they have today.

The ancient store building was heated with one old wood-burning heater and did not even boast a private outhouse. When nature called, we had to walk to the community toilet behind Ogden's Dime Store. This public rest station gave a new meaning to the word "dirty." Believe me, you don't know dirty if you never made an emergency stop at that place!

In between two failed business ventures, Dad rented out a small space in front of the building to a man and woman who, late one afternoon, arrived in Huntsville, pulling a small trailer behind an old LaSalle sedan. On the trailer, covered with a tattered tarpaulin, was one of those carnival type "one-minute studios." For only ten cents, a customer received three photographs—same pose—just slightly larger than a postage stamp.

The couple paid five dollars for two weeks' rent and unloaded the green leatherette covered "studio." It seemed they were doing a good business. Dad rose to the bait and bought the machine for $300.

It became obvious very soon that I was to run the One-Minute Studio.

It made a few bucks. I remember one Sunday afternoon when "Slim Pickens" Wilson, Junior, and Aunt Martha made a public appearance at the movie theater—direct from KWTO, the country music radio station in Springfield, Missouri. The only station with more listeners in Northwest Arkansas than KWTO was WSM in Nashville, when they broadcast the *Grand Ole Opry* on Saturday nights.

I decided to open up the One-Minute Studio, hoping to pick up a few dimes from those who came to hear the famous radio stars.

I opened an hour before show time and snapped pictures till dark. When the crowd dispersed, I found I had taken in over twelve dollars.

We moved to Springdale in '38. There was no space available for me to operate the machine on a part time basis. We covered the machine with the same old tarp and left it on the trailer.

Dad was working in the Palace Barber Shop one Saturday when Mr. Nelson came in. He asked if the photo machine was for sale. Dad told him he would like to get his money back. Mr. Nelson counted out the full payment of three hundred dollars in small bills.

At that time we were living with my grandparents in Spring Valley. We were still looking for a house we could afford in Springdale. That night, we drove slowly along the rough dirt road. Soon after we passed through Sonora, I saw a bright flash come from the ditch on my right. I heard a loud report, and a small hole appeared in our windshield, just below the rear view mirror. Someone had watched the cash transaction and was waiting for us. He knew the barber shop closed at nine, and we should pass some twenty to thirty minutes later. We made a fast exit in the old 1935 Plymouth.

Shortly after buying the little photo machine, Mr. Nelson died. Mrs. Nelson was middle-aged, overweight, and totally inexperienced in photography. She rented the small east room of the Concord Theater building, west of the Pioneer Lumber Company. For the next ten years she made a living with the "three for a dime" photo machine. She not only made a living, but sent her two sons through the University of Arkansas.

Mrs. Nelson had a secret: optimism, hard work, long hours, honesty, and a cheerful attitude. Many business men today could learn a lot from her.

I walked across Emma to the Pioneer and bought enough material to build a workbench, a counter, and some shelving. The cost was slightly over sixty dollars. The total bill included a gallon of light gray paint and a quart of green for trimming counters and shelves. My order was delivered within the hour. I could not afford a carpenter; I would do my own building and painting.

In 1946, knotty pine was in vogue. I joined the world of bad taste when I constructed my eight-foot work bench from the material. I gave it the usual two coats of orange shellac. Amid the attractive grey and green fixtures, the workbench stood out like the proverbial sore thumb. Totally inappropriate for a radio shop, it was "hell for stout" (strong) and very functional. I used it until I closed the shop thirty-five years later.

It took me five days to build and paint my workbench and fixtures. When completed, I stood in front of the store, admiring my handiwork. Though the shelves and tables were bare, I thought it looked attractive and businesslike.

Now that I was in the radio business, I realized I needed a service truck. Mr. Late, sympathetic to my needs, agreed to trade me a brand new Chevrolet panel truck for only four hundred dollars and my Fleetline Chevrolet. I quickly agreed; the trade was more than fair. I could use the panel truck as both a passenger car and a business vehicle.

Because of material shortages, the first panel trucks delivered after the war came equipped with a single seat for the driver, quite similar to those found in bread or milk trucks today. I didn't realize this when we traded. Fortunately, I located a bench-type, leather covered Ford seat that had been removed from a new station wagon when it was converted into an ambulance. The seat, intended for a smaller automobile, was far too narrow. When installed, a space of eight inches existed between the right door and seat. Less than two years later Mary and I drove the truck on our honeymoon. She never complained about the seat; she was sitting so close to me there was a lot of unused seat space to her right.

My empty store looked good enough, but if I were to earn a living, I must get it stocked. As I was starting a new business, my credit line was low; I could not depend on the banks for a substantial amount of financing. My plan was to buy a few parts, then try to earn enough repairing radios to gradually add inventory at a later date.

Our nearest wholesale radio supply was Wise Radio in Fort Smith. Elmo Wise, with his wife Bessie, operated a small business from their home in the 1000 block of Towson Avenue. The morning after I took delivery of my new truck, I left for Fort Smith. The weather looked threatening. I left about daylight; I didn't want to be caught in a snowstorm coming back across the mountain.

I arrived at Wise Radio a few minutes after eight. Elmo, alone in the store at this early hour, greeted me warmly. "Hi, I'm Elmo Wise," he said, brushing back a lock of brown hair. "I don't think I know you. Have you been in the store before?" I noticed he was rather heavy-set and appeared to be in his late thirties. I guessed he was a year or so too old to have seen service during the war.

"I'm Bruce Vaughan," I replied. "No, we haven't met. I'm opening up a radio repair shop in Springdale. I would like to buy a few parts, some test equipment, and perhaps open an account with you."

"Well, now, you should do good. I hear Coy Cantrell is talking of moving to the West Coast," he said. "Seems his son Dick is going to school there. Of course, the goin' may be rough for awhile. We still ain't gettin' but a trickle of parts, and test equipment is in short supply. I received one tube tester yesterday. It's a Triplett and sells for $69.95. I could let you have it."

"I'll take it," I answered. "How about a VOM? I've got an old meter I bought before the war, but it's not very good."

"Sorry, I am afraid you'll have to make it do for awhile. We are only gettin' a piece of equipment now and then. I guess it takes a while to switch back to makin' civilian goods after being in war production so long. It is almost impossible to find parts. I'll show you what I have."

We walked through what had been the living room of the old residence, picking up a few resistors, condensers, some solder and a soldering iron, a couple of Rider's manuals, dial cord, glue, a few volume controls, two speakers, and some assorted hardware. When I went to pay, I was shocked to find I had spent almost $160. After paying the bill, I was left with exactly $37.50 in the bank.

"Have you any ideas to help me get a start?" I asked. "Other than what I bought here today, I don't have anything but a few hand tools and the old meter I bought while a student at Spartan Aircraft School."

"Why don't you drop by Hunt's Appliance Store, down on Garrison?" replied Elmo. "They've been in business for years, and I know they've not had a radio repairman since 1940. I'll bet their storeroom is full of inoperative trade-ins they accumulated before their supply of new radios dried up. You could junk out the rough ones and repair the rest. This would give you a few sets to sell and some used parts to tide you over until you can do better. People understand that new parts are scarce. Just tell 'em the facts—that you can get their set going with what you have."

I thanked Elmo for his help and advice, then left the store. I looked at the sky; the weather seemed to be clearing. Glancing at my watch, I was pleased to see it was only 11:00 A.M. I decided to grab a quick lunch at the White Spot before going by Hunt's. A large hamburger steak covered with onions, French fries, Texas toast, and coffee cost me seventy-five cents.

I walked into the appliance department of Hunt's Department Store. A salesman approached. "And what can I do for you today?" he asked.

"I thought you might have some old, inoperative radios for sale," I replied.

I thought the salesman was going to kiss me.

"Just how many would you like to buy?" he asked. Leading the way into a back room, he pointed to a wall. "There they are. Take your pick for five bucks."

There must have been twenty dusty old radios, at least eight of which were large console models. Radios like that would bring a good price—if I could get them working. There was even a 1938 radio-phonograph combination.

I took out my bank book, studied the balance the way I thought a businessman man should, then said, "Tell you what . . . I'll give you $37.50 for the lot . . . good, bad, or junk. No questions, no complaints, no returns. I'll even load them myself."

"Fella, you just bought yourself a load of radios," replied the salesman.

Well, now I had no place to go but up. I had spent every last cent in my bank account.

It was not easy getting so many sets into the small panel wagon. I wanted to get them to my shop without damage. A stack of cardboard boxes in the alley behind the appliance store saved the day. Cutting them up with my pocket knife, I used the corrugated board as packing material around the better units. When all the sets were finally on board, I was surprised to find I had spent three hours in the store and in getting my truck loaded. I drove directly from Garrison Avenue to my shop in Springdale. I would have stopped along the road for a hamburger, but with less than five dollars in my pocket, I forgot that idea.

It was a few minutes past six o'clock when I backed up to the door of my shop. The Chevrolet garage and most other business houses on Emma had closed for the day. Feeling quite proud of my first stock of radios, I carefully unloaded them, then drove home to supper. My dad and mother had already finished eating. I quickly ate a plate of leftovers and returned to the shop to appraise my day's acquisitions.

The hours seemed to fly by. Though tired, I thoroughly enjoying troubleshooting the old radios. By 1:00 A.M. three nice console radios were ready for the showroom floor. One set, a large 1939 Zenith, was a real beauty. Its 12-inch speaker produced a rich, deep tone. I knew it would not last long before someone took it home with them. I applied a heavy coat of furniture polish to the three sets, rubbing them until they looked like new.

> *The propensity to truck, barter and exchange one thing for another . . . is common to all men, and to be found in no other race of animals.*
>
> ADAM SMITH (1723–1790)
> SCOTTISH ECONOMIST

I opened my shop at six the following morning, beating the rest of the downtown merchants by thirty minutes. Normally, the "broom brigade" (downtown store owners) showed up between six-thirty and a quarter to seven. After first sweeping the sidewalk, then their places of business, almost all downtown stores opened their doors for business at seven.

Only those who lived through the immediate post-war era can understand the business climate at that time. Practically no nonessential, and not nearly enough essential, merchandise was available to the retail trade after Pearl Harbor. The changeover from wartime to peacetime production took longer than people anticipated. Raw materials, as well as machine tools, were difficult to obtain. Finally, after many months, the production facilities of our country gained momentum. Industry awoke, slowly at first, then stretched a bit, and like a sleeping giant arose to its full height, larger and stronger than that of any other nation in the world.

For a period of three years or so, production was far behind demand. During this time a merchant could sell almost anything. It seemed there were waiting lists for everything. This was especially true of home appliances, radios, automobiles, and other large ticket items.

I noticed that other merchants seemed to have better sales of certain items if they displayed them on the sidewalk. I carried the big Zenith up front, placing it on the sidewalk just outside my door. A hand-lettered sign on top of the nice Zenith proclaimed that for the low price of only ninety-five dollars you could be its proud owner. With the aid of a long extension cord I soon had the radio playing loud enough to annoy the loafers in front of a beer joint down the street. A few of the more curious ambled up to see what the commotion was. I sold the set that day. The following day, the General Electric sold for sixty-five dollars. Not bad for a $37.50 investment—and I still had over a dozen sets left. I decided that if I advertised in our weekly paper, *The Springdale News,* I might sell even more. Quite suddenly, I was no longer broke; I had over $150 in my billfold.

ROY NIXON (SEPTEMBER 1993)

I opened my studio the last week of January 1941. I had been in the printing business in Prairie Grove. The small weekly paper was not making me a living. Photography had been a hobby of mine for years, and I decided to see if I could make a living at it.

My studio was upstairs over Barrack's Grocery. Mr. Barrack liked to drag stuff outside and display it on the sidewalk where it might sell better.

The city had some sort of ordinance at the time about merchants putting their wares on the sidewalk. When they told him he would have to discontinue the practice, he just tore the front of his building out and moved it back three feet.

"Now, let's see you stop me," he said. "As long as my merchandise is no more than three feet from my front window, it is on my property." The front of the building is still back three feet from the sidewalk.

Advertising was as rare as interesting news items in our weekly paper. Not many new businesses were opening, and old established firms felt there was no real need to advertise; everyone knew where they were. The population of our city in 1946 was about 1,800. The main business district was along Emma Avenue, starting at Highway 71 on the west and ending at the Jones Truck Lines terminal and offices on the east. Approximately 80% of the city's business firms was confined to this small area. Springdale's business district remained largely unchanged for fifty years. Of course, business firms came, went, and changed hands, but there was no major change until 1950.

As population grew after the war, the number of business firms grew proportionately. Old established stores wanted to expand. In the early post-war years there was just no place for a new business to open up. Eventually, business broke the bounds of Emma Avenue. Trying to keep a growing town confined to such a small area was like trying to harness a mighty ocean wave with a chain. The logical place to move was to "the highway." Up until the late 1940s, business along Highway 71 through Springdale was mostly limited to service stations, automobile dealers, tourist courts (the term motel was not yet in widespread use), and small cafes. Of course there were exceptions: Clyde Murphy's Flower Shop and Lindley Trucking, for example.

I would be amiss if I did not mention Jim Reis, the pickle king. Jim bought pickles by the barrel, repacked them in gallon jars, then sold to restaurants in the area. Jim's pickle operation was located one block south of the old Red Pig, now Jake's.

Some of the pioneers who ventured forth into the relatively unproven business climate of "the highway" were Harvard Harp, Harold Hewitt, Hal Brogdon, A. J.

Kennan, Milburn Neill, J. W. Eoff, Reid Holiman, Dwight Collins, Roy Ritter, W. C. Rogers, Sam Peace, and, in 1955, Bruce Vaughan. But I am getting ahead of my story . . . It is still 1946 and I have decided to advertise in *The Springdale News.*

You can bet that I had a rep from the *News* in my shop within minutes after calling the office. As I remember, it was Lem Groom who came to write up my first ad.

His first question stopped me cold. "Junior, what are you going to call your business?"

Somehow, that is something I had never thought of. I suppose I did need a name for it. This shows the depth and planning that had gone into my endeavor.

"Well . . . er . . . let's see . . . I suppose it should have something to do with radio," I answered.

I must have shown some expression when Lem called me Junior. It was a name I detested. I had often said that if I ever had so many kids I couldn't think of names for 'em, I would number 'em before I saddled one with the name of Junior. During the war I had been called either Vaughan or Sarge.

I will be forever grateful to Lem for asking his next question. "Do you like being called Junior?"

"As a matter of fact, no. I have tried to figure out a way to stop people from calling me that for years," I answered, "but nothing seems to work."

"I'll guarantee you this: if you will call this place Bruce's 'something or other,' within a year no one will ever call you Junior again," said Lem.

"Do you really think so?" I asked.

"Give it a try and you'll see," answered Lem. "I had a suspicion that you would like to unload the Junior thing—and this will work."

"Okay," I answered. "How does 'Bruce's Radio Shop' sound?" You can see the originality and daring I was bringing into the business climate of Springdale.

"I dunno . . . you might want to sell appliances or maybe even television someday—if they ever get all the bugs worked out of it. Why not 'Bruce's Electric Shop?' With that name you could sell just about anything that ran on batteries or plugged into the wall." Lem was writing on a scratch pad all the time he was talking.

"That sounds good to me," I answered. "I do plan on selling some appliances and going into sound equipment. Yes, let's call it 'Bruce's Electric Shop.'"

Through the years the nature and name of the business changed, but Lem was right. Within very few months everyone stopped calling me Junior.

At this point some readers may wish to turn to the Appendix which follows Chapter 7 for an account of the origins and development of radio and television and of the early attempts to provide these sources of entertainment and knowledge to Springdale. The account of Emma Avenue's business characteristics and development continues in Chapter 4.

CHAPTER 4

The First Two Years

It is well-known what a middleman is; he is a man who
bamboozles one party and plunders the other.

BENJAMIN DISRAELI (1804–1881)
ENGLISH PRIME MINISTER

"I have those hard to find volt-and-a-half tubes," said a voice behind me. I was unaware of the salesman's presence. Today, one of our first warm spring days, was reason enough to have the front door open.

Pushing aside the little Stewart Warner AC-DC set I was working on, I looked at him and asked, "What tubes are you talking about? They are all hard to find."

"You know . . ." he answered, "battery-type tubes. I have complete sets: 1A7, 1N5, 1H5, and 3Q5. The tube line-up used in thousands of farm-pack radios. Brand new, JAN (Joint Army-Navy) tubes, and I am sellin' em' for only eight dollars a set."

I didn't want him to know how inexperienced I was about the repair business. Truthfully, I didn't know if those were tubes I would be needing. So far, my business was so slow that I hadn't encountered a need for any of the tubes he mentioned. I bought four sets—just in case—and counted out thirty-two of my hard earned bucks.

Less than three months later, I regretted not floating a loan and buying a hundred sets of the tubes.

In 1946, Rural Electrification Authority lines had yet to reach the majority of farm families in Northwest Arkansas. Construction of electric lines, started in 1939, stopped abruptly after Pearl Harbor. Literally hundreds of farm families owned battery-powered radios; almost all used this tube line-up.

One of our best sellers, in the late 1940s, was the so-called "1,000 hour" battery pack. Both Burgess and Philco had trucks that worked this area every two weeks. Because of the weight of batteries, a considerable saving could be had by buying "off the truck." In 1946, I sold my batteries for $4.45. By 1949 they were selling for $5.95. In 1952, they sold for $7.50. By 1955 the sales of batteries and battery-powered radios became nonexistent. Now REA reached even the most remote farms.

Like other ex-servicemen, I was accustomed to military schedules, working long hours day or night. Eight-hour days had very little meaning to members of the Armed Forces. I often was in the shop before daylight. It was a good time to work. A cup of hot coffee on the work bench, the acrid smell of a 100-watt soldering iron wafting through the still air of the shop, and Glenn Miller or Tommy Dorsey music coming from a radio playing softly in the background created a comfortable environment. I felt cozy, secure, pleased with the world, and better able to concentrate on difficult repair jobs. Soon the street noise would start, and the spell would be broken, but for the present all was quiet and peaceful.

On one such morning, unable to sleep, I opened the shop at 4:00 A.M. Crime in Springdale was next to nonexistent, so the thought of being in a store alone at that hour was not a cause for concern.

I glanced up from the little AC-DC Arvin I was working on. A young man in Army uniform was looking in my front window. The front door was unlocked; I motioned him to come in.

Curious as to why anyone would be on the street at this hour, I offered him a cup of coffee. Perhaps he would tell me why he was window-shopping at 4:00 A.M., three hours before most downtown stores opened.

"I just got off the bus," he said. "I've been riding all night. I was discharged at Jefferson Barracks yesterday. A cup of hot coffee would sure taste good."

"Where do you live?" I asked.

"My mom and dad live over on Park Street," he replied. "I noticed the little white RCA radio in your window. How much is it?"

"That's a used one," I replied. "We still can't get new radios. I've checked it out; it plays good. You can have it for twenty bucks."

"Okay, I'll take it," he said. "I wanted to bring Mom and Dad a little present. I didn't have a chance to buy them anything on the way home."

The incident did not seem at all unusual then. Armed robbery was not a serious threat in Springdale—that came later. Until the early 1940s our underpaid patrol officer, Lee Shankles, had little trouble keeping the peace. His duties were largely confined to arresting disorderly drunks. When it came to calming down unruly drunks, Lee had a way about him that seemed to work. He carried a night stick that was rumored to be filled with lead. He first placed the offender under arrest; then if the celebrant offered enough resistance, Lee swung his stick, hitting the offender in the side of the head. This seemed to have a soothing effect on the more violent types. On rare occasions a second blow might be required.

REUBEN BRYANT

I suppose you have heard the story they used to tell about Lee and the Bishop murders. When all the shooting started and the bodies began falling, the cry went out for our peace officer, Lee Shankles.

Someone found him in the Concord Theater lobby.

"Come quick, Lee! They are having a big shooting up the street. Two or three are dead already," his informant said.

"Do they have guns?" asked Lee.
"Yes, they have guns!" yelled the citizen. "We need you right away!"
"Are they still shooting?" asked Lee.
"Yes, they are still shooting," replied the exasperated citizen.
"Well, let's just wait a few more minutes," answered Lee. "Then we'll go have
a look."

After the war our city government realized the need to expand the police force. Headquarters was in the old city hall building (#62) on Spring Street. From WWII to the present we have been fortunate to have a first class, highly professional police department. Sometimes support from the city council was not all it should be, but the department continued to improve, using whatever funds were available.

Chief Wayne Hyden came to me inquiring about two-way radios for the department. He asked several questions: How much would it cost? What distance would the radios reach? What maintenance problems should the department expect? I explained to him that my knowledge of police radios was limited. However, I was sure Motorola would furnish me with all needed information; perhaps they would have one of their field engineers give a presentation to the city council.

The chief suggested I get my paperwork together and present it to the council at their next meeting. If they seemed interested, he would have an engineer attend a future meeting.

I became enthused, made a few phone calls, and collected a sizeable amount of material. I arrived early for the council meeting, my brief case filled with information I thought would be of interest. When the chief asked me to present the information, one of the council members hooked his thumbs in the suspenders of his overalls, leaned back in his chair, and announced, "This council is not interested in buying two-way radios. They are not needed and would be a unnecessary expense." The rest of the council quickly agreed; they didn't dare buck the influential council member. I could see the disappointment on the chief's face. It's difficult to stop progress. Within a few months it became obvious that the police department must have a means of communication. They got their much needed radios. Layman Smith of Smith Communications in Fayetteville made the sale, doing all the installation work himself. I never submitted a bid. When I saw Smith putting up the tall, lightweight tower on top of the old church building, I was really glad I lost the sale. He earned much more than he was paid. I don't mean to imply serious crime was nonexistent in those days; we had our share of killings. Before the war, three people were killed in one incident. The shooting occurred in front of a cafe in "beer joint row." Shortly after the war, while the pool hall was located in the old Opera House building, one man was killed in an argument. One of the fellows, using a pool cue for a club, delivered a lethal blow to his opponent. A few doors west of my shop, a shooting occurred during a poker game. While the shooting was an accident, it did little to improve the reputation of the block. If you used a certain amount of discretion and common sense, you were not in danger. There is nothing to be gained from going into the details of such incidents. If you are curious, the stories are well-documented in *The Springdale News.*

Christmas of '46 came; business was fair—and I received an unexpected present. Mr. Late gave me notice to vacate his building in January. I never understood why. He was very cordial and continued to give me terrific deals on cars and trucks. He just wanted me out, so he could padlock the empty building. Cooper Jewelry, located in the old liquor store building (#76), was having a "close out" sale. Mr. Cooper told me he wanted to move his jewelry store back to his hometown of Ozark. I offered him a small amount—forty dollars, if I remember correctly—for his investment in fixtures. He, in turn, let me assume his lease. The only thing I received of value in the deal was his old regulator clock. I still have it in my home. On January 15, he vacated the building.

My moving expense was small. Jimmy King, a wizened old man who picked up grocery money by doing odd jobs up and down the block, moved my stock in his wheelbarrow. It was his idea. He heard I was moving and came by to see me.

"I can move everything you have in here in my wheelbarrow. Well, maybe not the shelves and tables, but everything else," he said.

As I was only moving from 220 to 206 East Emma, I figured I could get one man to help me carry all the larger items. There was really not all that much.

Jimmy worked all morning, making trip after trip with his old wooden wheelbarrow full of small items. By nightfall my entire inventory was in the new home of Bruce's Electric Shop. We opened for business the following morning.

Jim was one of Springdale's more colorful characters. He was better known as "Sweet Potato Jim." The origin of the nickname is best left unwritten.

Harold Dean Hewitt was well-known along Emma as a "soft touch." He never refused help to anyone. Every morning he paid Jim to burn the contents of his liquor store's waste baskets. If Jim needed a little extra cash, Harold would let him wash the windows.

At one time Jim was in the manufacturing business. He owned the largest coat hanger manufacturing plant in town. During WWII, when almost everything was impossible to get, Tom Warren ran out of coat hangers for his Bon Ton Cleaners. Jimmy heard of his problem. He hurried home, made a few hangers, and took them to Mr. Warren.

"I can deliver all these you need," he said. A price was agreed upon, and Jimmy was in business.

Jimmy placed a coat hanger in the center of a old wooden table, traced its outline with a lead pencil, then drove nails every inch along the outline. This was his jig for forming wire. He hit up a bargain with The Famous Hardware for several hundred feet of "grape" wire and went into the coat hanger business. He wound the wire around the pattern of nails, gave it a few twists, and had a passable war-time coat hanger. Tom took his entire output.

I liked my new location. Two doors west was Dodson's Five and Ten. Dodson's lunch counter, staffed by Mida Harrison (Neff) and Mary Frances Maestri, soon became my favorite place for coffee. Both Mida and Mary were attractive young ladies. I had known Mida for years—since well before the war. I wasted little time getting to know Mary Frances.

Several weeks later (February 13, 1947), I got up enough courage to ask her for a date. She accepted.

Mary told me that night that she planned to leave her job in the dime store very soon. She had been offered a job at the First National Bank, but didn't have enough self-confidence to accept. In her own words, "I'm just not smart enough to work in the bank." Her plans were to join friends in California and look for work there.

It was obvious—here was a problem requiring immediate action. The following day, St. Valentine's Day 1947, I stopped by Coger's Drug. Cliff Samuel and I had been friends since our days at dear old H. S. V. S. (Huntsville State Vocational School). Clifford drove the old Model A Ford school bus from Clifty to the newly built vocational school.

"Cliff, I want to buy one of those Parker 51 fountain pens they are advertising so much," I said.

"I've got 'em, Bruce, but the doggone things are expensive," replied Cliff. "One will set you back about twenty-five bucks. I've got cheaper pens that will do the same thing."

"Nope," I answered, "I'll take the Parker. It's going to take some drastic action if my plan is to work. Can you gift wrap it for me?"

"Sounds like your head is made up," answered Cliff. "I'll wrap it up for you."

CLIFFORD SAMUEL (September 1993)

I moved to Springdale in 1940 and went to work for Mr. Coger in the drug store.

Mr. and Mrs. Coger were going to Kansas City to have complete medical check-ups in the clinic there. Clay Carter was working for Coger then. I was supposed to stay five or six weeks, helping Clay run the store. After six weeks, nothing was said about my quitting. I never returned to Clifty to live; I stayed almost forty years.

Mr. Coger opened the drug store in 1921. I stayed with him from 1940 until he closed in 1978.

Judge Guy Howard walked to town every morning. He always stopped at Joyce's to buy a cigar, then came down to Coger's for a coke. He was very impatient. As quick as he stepped up to the fountain, he would start hammering on it with a coin. You had to wait on him immediately, or he would leave. Those nickel cokes are what paid our overhead.

If you remember, he always wore that wide-brimmed hat, a white shirt, and white shoes. One morning he came in the store wearing one white shoe and one brown shoe.

I look down at his feet and asked, "What happened, Judge?"

He replied, "Oh, that little cocker spaniel of mine . . . I guess he drug one of my white shoes off somewhere. I looked and looked for it. I finally gave up and put on one of my brown shoes. I don't really care what anyone thinks, anyway."

I laughed and said, "You know, Judge, you could have worn both of the brown shoes."

Judge Howard looked thoughtful. After some time he replied, "You know, Cliff, I never thought of doing that."

My next stop was Lichlyter's. Leo Lichlyter sold me a nice Valentine card. Louis Lichlyter was busy at work unpacking merchandise. I stopped and visited with him a few minutes before returning to my shop.

I gave considerable thought to the message I wrote on the Valentine card, urging Mary to accept the job at the First National Bank. Then, armed with card and gift-wrapped pen, I drove the panel truck to John Downum's flower shop and greenhouse on West Emma.

"Mr. Downum," I said, "I want you to deliver a dozen red roses to Mary Frances Maestri. She works behind the lunch counter at Dodson's, or you can deliver them to her home. She lives in the first house east of the church at Tontitown."

"I'll take care of it," he said. "Flowers have gone up a little; that will be $7.50 plus tax."

"Fine. I would like for her to get the flowers today," I answered. I handed Mr. Downum the card and the small gift-wrapped box. "Here's the card, and please put this gift in with the flowers."

On our next date, Mary told me she had accepted the position with the bank and would be working there after March 1. I'll never know if it was the flowers, the Parker 51, or the card that changed her mind.

Mary loved her new job from the beginning. Her fears were completely unfounded. The First National was a great place to work. Employees were: Lee Sanders, president; Faye Stafford, vice president; Ewell Fitzgerald, cashier and teller; Bonnie Hanks, head bookkeeper and teller; John Rose, John Allen, Billie Jines, tellers; and Jean Keever, Yolanda Nunn (Late), Mary Maestri (Vaughan), and Georgia Mae Newton, bookkeepers.

Lee Sanders considered the bank employees a family. He never missed a chance to invite the entire crew out to eat. It seemed there was a social evening or party at least once a month.

Mary told me how Lee Sanders would often extend a small loan to customers who had no collateral, taking the money from his personal bank account. He never told those customers their credit would not pass the bank requirements; he just underwrote the loan himself.

In those days before computers, bookkeeping was not easy for a bank. Every night the books had to total, or the entire staff returned after supper and stayed until the error was found. I remember Mary's working to well past 10:00 P.M. many nights.

On one occasion it was much later and continued for several nights. One of the teller windows came up short $500—quite a large sum in those years. The money could not be found. Such was the trust of all employees that the incident was considered a mystery, not embezzlement by one of the staff.

Several weeks later the mystery was solved. A large open box of adding machine paper was stored on a shelf under the cash drawer at the teller window. When one of the employees reached for a roll of paper, he was surprised to find the five hundred-dollar bills, held together with a paper clip. Apparently the money, on top of a stack of bills in the drawer, slipped over the back of the drawer and fell into the box of adding machine paper. The books were again in balance.

ESPEN WALTERS (September 1993)

George Ownbey was a good friend of mine. I always thought a lot of George even if he did tend to drink a little too much at times. I remember on one occasion when Lee Shankles threw George in jail. That's when the city hall and jail were in the basement of the old church, just north of the cleaners there on Mill Street.

When George sobered up, Lee let him out of jail so he could raise his bond or fine money—I forget which.

George walked up to the First National Bank and asked to see Lee Sanders. Mr. Sanders listened to his story and said, "George, I'll be glad to loan you the money, but you will need a co-signer. Go down and see if Espen will sign for you."

When George explained his problem to me, I said, "George, you run back up to the bank and tell Lee Sanders that I'll loan you the money, if he will co-sign your note. I never heard any more about it. I'll bet Lee let him have the money."

Arkansas Radio, a Little Rock company, was the state distributor for Philco. Very few lines of merchandise were sold on a "factory direct" basis. Everything was two-stepped: manufacturers selling to state distributors (so-called middlemen) and they, in turn, selling to the retailing dealers. This outmoded distributor system added at least 20% to the cost of most large ticket items. Some distributors, especially in times of merchandise shortages, applied all sorts of pressure to small dealers.

In the fall of 1947, Frank Flynn, the manager of Arkansas Radio came by my shop. I knew this must be a special occasion. Normally, the "big wheels" remained in their offices. Salesmen made dealer calls, especially to small dealers like me. After the usual greetings Frank suggested we go next door for a cup of coffee. "I have something to tell you that you are not going to believe," he said. "Philco has invented a record that will play for thirty minutes on each side. Now, what do you think of that?"

Well, of course, I was skeptical. My mind skipped back to 1938 . . .

Philco announced the famous "beam of light" phonograph pickup. All major magazines carried advertising for this amazing development—the record player that plays on a beam of light with no wire connection between the record and the radio. The advertising made it sound great. In the 1930s, The Famous Hardware sold both Zenith and Philco radios. I remember watching one of The Famous employees give a demonstration to a customer.

"Just imagine," the salesman said, turning up the volume as a record played on the Philco console, "every sound you hear is carried on a little beam of light." The amusing thing about watching this demonstration was that neither salesman or customer realized they had been conned by big business.

Sure, the music travelled on a beam of light. Inside the massive head on the record pickup was a light bulb and lens, arranged to focus a beam of light on a mirror attached to the needle. Light reflected off the mirror was picked up by a photoelectric cell, also in the pickup head. Anyone can easily see that all this added a lot of weight to the pickup, thus damaging any record played on the machine. If the efficiency of this mess approached 100%, which is impossible, the sound achieved would be about the same as the crystal pickup it replaced. The frequency response of 78 RPM records was so limited that almost any crystal pickup was capable of reproducing more than was on the record. The idea was obviously impractical because of cost and weight. So much for reverse engineering . . .

> *Let the great world spin forever down the ringing grooves of change.*
>
> LORD TENNYSON (1809–1892)
> ENGLISH POET

I worked for The Famous Hardware about six weeks—from the time I graduated the last of May until mid-July. I quit when Ed and I could not agree on my salary. I wanted ten dollars a week; Mr. Cummings wanted me to work for five; and Clark-Deaver offered me twelve.

When I think of The Famous Hardware, I remember a day in June 1939. On this fine summer day, The Famous became famous—from one end of Emma Avenue to the other. On this day, the installation of Springdale's very first intercommunications system was completed in the largest hardware store in the area. The Famous was the only three-story retail store in town. In addition to the three floors, there was a huge "L" shaped warehouse behind the store. A very real need existed for a method of communicating with the many different departments. The first floor of The Famous was for paint and hardware; the second floor was for furniture, radios, and floor covering; and the top floor was primarily storage. It was also the floor where large items were unpacked and made ready for the floor.

On the week in question, we had just received a carload of cast iron stoves—large wood heaters and cookstoves. Dale Reed and I were on the third floor, unpacking and assembling the stoves. The stoves came in a near knock-down condition, packed in wooden crates. It was a two-hour job getting one unpacked and ready for show.

Ed Cummings was known by his employees for his uncanny sales ability with the farm trade. Dale and I were working away, listening to the sounds coming over the newly installed speaker. We could hear every word from the first floor.

"Well, hello there, Jim," we heard Ed say. "Tell me, how is your crop this year?"

Before the customer could reply, Ed was talking again. "How are your wife and those fine kids? I sure would like to see them. I'll bet those fine boys are a real help on the farm."

Speakers all over the store came alive: "Well, there is another farmer about to buy more than he can pay for." The words echoed throughout the building. Employees gasped, customers looked astonished, and Mr. Ed was livid with rage. A speaker somewhere in the store, one of the remotes, was switched to talk instead of listen. The words were loud and clear; the intercom was working fine. Luckily, the culprit was never identified.

My mind returned to the present. I took a long drink of coffee, turned back to Frank, and said, "Tell me this—how do they expect to get all that music on one record?"

Frank went on to explain that this would be called a LP record—twelve inches in size. It would sound better, with less needle pressure, than anything on the market. They were able to do all this because the grooves were closer together— microgrooves, Frank called them. As "the" Philco dealer in Springdale, I was in on the "ground floor" of this startling discovery. I had not, at this time, learned about electronic distributors and their "franchises."

I caught the excitement and ordered a dozen of the special record-playing attachments Philco was introducing. There were no records on the market that would play on the attachments, so Philco provided us with a demonstration record to advertise and to sell for only $1.95.

Strangely enough, I sold all the LP attachments for $29.95 each. Customers wanted to be the first to own something new. Their investment was safe; within weeks a few LP records began to appear in record shops.

Now, years later, I find this story amusing. I can visualize every distributor, of every major line in the United States, handing their dealers the same line of bull. I do not know who really developed the LP record. In this area Philco was first on the market, and I was the first dealer in Springdale to sell equipment that would play the new records.

My exclusive did not last long; within the year every dealer in Springdale had LP equipment for sale.

Mary Frances Maestri and I were married December 15, 1947. After a short honeymoon we moved into a small apartment at 615 Allen Street. At the time I had a fifteen year old high school student working part time in the shop. His goal was to learn enough radio to get a ham license. He came in after school and Saturdays to help with small jobs—mostly checking tubes, sweeping out, and keeping the front windows clean. Before leaving for the honeymoon, I decided to have him open the shop on Saturday. I planned on returning Sunday afternoon.

I had several completed radio repair jobs in the shop waiting to be picked up. I found, early on, that most customers would not complain if you took four or five days to repair their radios, as long as it was not over a weekend. Come what may, they wanted their radios by Saturday night. On Saturday nights, half of the radios in Washington County were tuned to the *Grand Ole Opry* on WSM, Nashville.

My last order to my young employee was, "Please, please, don't forget to lock up at night. Whatever else you forget, remember to lock the door."

He left it open. Someone went in the store and waited around a while, thinking I had stepped out for something. When no one returned, the customer decided I had forgotten to lock up and called the police. They drove by the young man's house, got the key, and locked up my shop. Nothing was missing from the store. This tells a lot about the type of town we had.

FALL 1949 . . .

I wondered how old the little cast-iron gas stove really was. A real antique, it was part of the deal I received when Cooper Jewelry moved out. On the front of the stove was a iron shelf for a coffee pot. When not in use, the decorative shelf folded up flat, appearing to be part of the ornate cast-iron filigree. I poured my mug full of steaming coffee.

Many Sundays, Mary and I drove out of town for lunch. Today, however, was a good day to stay home. Cold and overcast, it looked as though it might start snowing any minute. Mary went to bed with a book; I decided to go to the shop and work until time for dinner.

With coffee mug in hand, I stepped to the front of the store to see if it was snowing. The sky appeared lighter than it did when I came to work. I watched as a Pontiac sedan came down Emma from the west, made a "U" turn at the railroad tracks, and parked in front of the Bon Ton. The Pontiac was the only car parked in the block; my truck was behind the store. Howard "Nub" Clark stepped from his car, reached in the back seat, and took out his little Speed Graphic camera.

I remember when Howard bought the Speed Graphic; it was the summer of 1939. Yes, I remember . . .

To attract Saturday business back then, the merchants of Springdale contributed to a fund for a "Saturday drawing." For every dollar spent with one of the contributing merchants, customers received a ticket. Ticket holders had to be present at the drawing to win. If the money was unclaimed, it was carried over till the following week. The fund sometimes built up to a sizeable total. Of course, the bigger the prize, the larger the crowd attending.

The drawing had built up to over $500—enough to buy a new car or a kitchen full of new appliances. A record crowd was expected to be present in the old city park (site of our present administration building) for the drawing.

I was working for Clark-Deaver Hardware when Paul Jones delivered Howard's new camera. As he unpacked the Speed Graphic, we both commented about the beauty and precision of the little "press" camera.

Even buying a camera was news enough to warrant discussions around the tables in Penrod's. Within hours all the local coffee drinkers knew Howard had bought an "expensive" camera. Possession of such a camera carried with it a responsibility. It was decided over coffee that Howard should photograph the drawing on Saturday. The photos could be used for publicity. Howard was quick to agree; it would give him a chance to try out his wide-angle lens. A crowd of several hundred was expected.

Howard loaded several film holders with Super X film, went to the warehouse, brought out a ten-foot stepladder, loaded everything in the service truck, and then drove to the city park. As expected, over 300 people showed up for the drawing. The air was charged with excitement. Placing his stepladder west of the old bandstand so the sun would be at his back, Howard climbed to the top of the ladder to get a wide-angle shot of the event; he waited to record this special moment in time.

Up on the bandstand, the official in charge solemnly turned the crank on the wire cage; thousands of tickets tumbled again and again as the crowd looked on. Beside the wire cage a small girl waited, ready to insert her hand among the tickets and bring forth one that would be worth hundreds of dollars to some lucky person.

An elderly gentleman, dressed in faded overalls and white shirt, was more intrigued with Howard and his Speed Graphic than with the drawing. As silence blanketed the city park, his words to Howard went down in the lore of Emma Avenue:

"Young feller, iffn yore aimin' on gettin' a picher o' this here crowd, ur gonna need a bigger Kodak than thet un."

Many in the crowd heard the remark; Howard never quite lived it down. Every time he showed up with a camera, some joker would yell, "When you gonna get a bigger Kodak, Howard?"

I opened the door of my shop. "You need a bigger Kodak," I said.

Nub smiled, but never stopped working. He set up a tripod, attached the Graphic to the pan-head, and shot several pictures of the old Pioneer Lumber building. He moved up and down the street, getting different angles. When he finished, he came in the store.

"Guess you're curious about what I'm doing," he said. "Dupe (Dupree Deaver) and I are thinking about merging our Hardware with the Pioneer. If we do, we are trying to decide how much of the old building is worth saving. It would need extensive remodeling. That's the reason for all the pictures. By the way, I would just as soon everyone in town did not know about this until our plans are final."

"I thought you were going to build on the old 'Brushwood' Nelson property," I replied. "It was in *The Springdale News* some time ago that you were building a new store there."

"We decided it was too far off the main drag," answered Nub. "We will probably sell it."

Howard reached in his coat pocket and took out a well-worn briar pipe. Then he reached for his tin of Brigg's tobacco. He carried it in his left shirt pocket. With slow, thoughtful deliberation he filled the old pipe and lit it with a kitchen match.

I also smoked a pipe; however, I preferred Sir Walter Raleigh. I tried Brigg's a few times, but stuck with my Sir Walter.

"Nub, I know your daddy was a pipe smoker. Can you remember what kind of tobacco he used?" I asked.

"No. You know, Bob and I were pretty young when Dad (Robert Clark Sr.) died. I wish we could have had him around a little longer."

ROBERT "BOB" H. CLARK (AUGUST 1993)

You know Maudine Farish; she worked at The Springdale News for years. Some years ago she married T. C. Sanders. Well, every time I see Maudine or hear her name, I remember the night Dad died. A couple of years ago Maudine told me her side of this story—so it is all true.

It was Christmas Eve, 1924. I had a date—I don't remember the girl's name, but her dad was an insurance agent, and they lived up on Johnson Street.

Well, anyway, I had asked Dad if I could use the car that night. I was going to my date to the show at the Concord. After the show we planned on stopping at the drugstore for a soda Dad said, "Well, OK, Son—you can have the car, but before you two go to the movie, drop by The Famous and give me a ride home."

I picked my girl up, and we drove downtown. I parked in front of The Famous. Remember this was before it moved. It was still on the corner of Spring and Emma.

It was nearing seven o'clock; the streets were almost deserted. Dad came out of the store and locked the front door. Ed and the rest of the help had already gone home to be with their families on Christmas Eve.

Dad had just got the door locked and started for the car, when a car pulled in beside me. It was Mr. Farish, Maudine's father.

"Bob, I sure hate to bother you on Christmas Eve, but Maudine has her heart set on that little rocking chair in your front window. I have decided to add it to her Christmas presents, if you would not mind opening up and selling it to me.

I tried to get here earlier, but got tied up—you know how that goes," said Mr. Farish.

"Not at all, not at all," said Dad. "I'll be glad to open up for you. I want Maudine to have a good Christmas."

After Mr. Farish had left with the little rocking chair, Dad got in the back seat of the car. I backed out and started up Emma toward our house on North Thompson.

"Bob, I'm not feeling so good," said Dad. "Is your mother home?"

"No, Dad, Mother has gone to the First Baptist Church," I answered. "They are having a Christmas program tonight. She was going to help pass out the presents and candy."

Dad was a relatively young man. I didn't feel there was cause for alarm, even though he again told me he felt bad and asked about Mother.

We went in the house. I helped him feed the old wood stove; then Dad pulled up his favorite rocker and put his feet against the nickel-plated rail alongside the stove.

My date and I drove back downtown to the Concord. After the movie we parked the car in front of Ownbey's, got out of the car, and started into the drug store.

Mr. Ownbey stepped out of the store and met me in the middle of the sidewalk. "Bob," he said, "I've got some bad news for you. Bob, your dad died tonight."

I thought someone had hit me in the back of head. I was so shocked—I had to grab hold of Garland to keep from falling flat on my face on the sidewalk.

He said, "Come on in. One of us will drive your date home and then take you home. You are in no condition to drive."

Well, we pieced the story together. Dad had apparently got to feeling worse and called Dr. Martin. Dr. Martin lived on Emma in what used to be the funeral home. As a matter of fact, Dr. Martin built that house.

"Bob," said Dr. Martin, "you just sit down and take it easy till I get there. I'll be right up."

It was only four blocks from the Martin house to ours. I would assume he was there in minutes. He knocked on the door, but there was no answer. Dr. Martin opened the door and stepped inside.

Dad was dead. He was sitting by the stove, one foot on the stove rail. Apparently he died very soon after calling Dr. Martin. The cause of death was a cerebral hemorrhage.

"Nub, I sure enjoyed working for Clark-Deaver Hardware. I was just thinking today about the time Vannes Boone went into Penrod's, and they were installing Springdale's first fluorescent lights. Do you remember?" I asked.

"I'll never forget it," answered Nub. "I never saw Vannes move that fast before."

It must have been in August of 1939—I remember it was a warm day. Vannes had taken a break to get a coke. He had only been gone a few minutes, when he came running back to the store.

"You've got to come see this," he exclaimed. "They are putting some new kind of lights in Penrod's. The bulbs are long glass tubes! The light they give off is unbelievable! It is already as bright inside as it is outside, and they are only half done."

Dupe and Vannes stayed in the store while Nub and I ran next door to see these amazing lights. We agreed; they were really something. I hurried back to the store, so Dupe could get a look at this miracle.

Mary and I moved into a small apartment on Allen Street. We had three rooms: a living room, a kitchen, and a room full of ham radio equipment. Our bed was in a corner of the radio room.

In the early months of 1949, the *Arkansas Gazette* carried a story in its Sunday paper about a fellow named Garner Carter, who lived on a mountain top near Altus. It seemed Mr. Carter had picked up a TV station in Boston. I decided to pay him a visit.

Yes, he had picked up Boston, Carter assured me. I listened with awe as he told of rare occasions when a picture would appear on the small-screen TV sitting in the corner of his living room. He went on to say that within months there would be a station on the air from Oklahoma City. Then he hoped for better results. It was rumored that Tulsa might also get a station. He sold me; I decided to buy a TV set.

On my way back to Springdale I stopped by Wise Radio in Ft. Smith. They had just received their first TV set, a seven-inch Hallicrafters. It was packaged in a nice two-tone grey metal cabinet and sold for $179.95 wholesale. I bought it.

Of course, a TV was worthless without a respectable antenna. I bought a freestanding tower and a stacked antenna. No rotor was needed. My only hope for a viewable picture was Oklahoma City or Tulsa—both in a westerly direction.

Mary was slightly perturbed. After all, I still had the ham station in the bedroom. When I heard last fall (1948) that both Joplin and Springfield were on the air with frequency modulation, I bought an FM tuner, 30-watt amplifier, and Jensen bass-reflex speaker. It fit nicely between the bed and the 500-watt ham transmitter. Now, we had a television in the bedroom. It looked like the bed might have to go.

When Jones Truck Lines delivered the antenna and tower, Mary agreed to help with the installation. Everything went well until she climbed up on the roof to help fish the "lead in" through the attic. I didn't know she was so terribly afraid of heights. It seemed easy enough going up the ladder, but she panicked when she started down. I thought for awhile I was going to have to set the house on fire to get her off the roof.

I kept the little Hallicrafters until May. Every night I turned the set on, never hearing a word or seeing a picture. I often imagined I could see some sort of picture in the snow, but nothing I could identify. How was I to know what a TV picture looked like? I had never seen one.

I decided it must be my set; I needed a more powerful one. I traded it back to

Wise Radio, and they ordered a RCA 630TS for me. This is the chassis, patented by RCA, that was used by the majority of television manufacturers in the late 1940s.

Friends of ours, Lewis and Janis Ingraham, drove up from Paris, Texas, for a week's visit. Lewis had worked for me for a short time when he and Janis were first married. Janis worked at the First State Bank. They moved back to Paris, their home town, where Lewis put in a radio shop. He bought a TV and with the help of a 100-foot-high antenna was able to pick up Dallas, more or less regularly. He spent two days checking out my installation and could find nothing wrong. We even lowered the tower and put on a new 300-ohm line—still no picture. We decided to take in a movie at the new Spot Theater in Siloam Springs.

Before leaving for the movie, Lewis turned to me and said, "I think I'll check the TV one more time; there might be a picture on it."

I heard him yell, "Come look at this, y'all! You're not going to believe it!"

We ran to the bedroom; WKY in Oklahoma City was as clear as a black-and-white glossy photograph. I rushed to the front yard and called to my neighbors, Harold and Dolly Henson, "Quick! Come over and see TV!"

Within twenty minutes the little apartment was full of people wanting to get their first look at television. Mary phoned Ellis Stafford of *The Springdale News,* but he was not home. Then she called friends in Tontitown. Some rushed to Springdale to see TV. Memo Morsani, a lover of opera, was disappointed. He decided he could live without this new miracle; there was no opera on TV that night.

WKY had started transmitting live TV programs, four hours a day, from 6 P.M. till 10 P.M. During this period everyone connected with the industry was in a learning process—station owners, engineers, dealers, and repairmen. If WKY had projection equipment, it was not ready for use. The live programs left a lot to be desired. One program I remember was *The Smoking Room.* A middle-aged gentleman, seated behind a small desk, puffed on a old briar pipe and gave forth with "down home" philosophy.

Bob Sanders of *The Springdale News* put a little blurb about my TV in his widely read "Springdalia" column.

BUCKET (MRS. MARTY) STAFFORD (1993)

Bob Sanders came to Springdale in 1946. The war was ending, and Bob was down at Camp Chaffee. Marty put an ad (Wanted-Advertising Salesman) in the paper. Bob read the ad and came to Springdale to talk to Marty. His daughter Beverly was three months old at the time.

Marty instantly liked Bob. They had so much in common, even the same birthday. Bob was a wonderful person. The longer Marty knew Bob the more he thought of him.

Bob wrote a column called "Springdalia." We were a weekly then. Later we published twice weekly. We kept adding a day at a time until the paper became a daily.

> *Almost every morning Bob would go down to Penrod's to gather bits of gossip for his column. Speaking of Penrod's—wasn't that a local institution? I can remember Marty and I sitting at a table, eating, and watching the young school kids have such a good time. They always preferred a booth to a table. I can picture Peggy Ann Watkins (Mrs. Stacy Looney) visiting with her friends in a booth. She was such a pretty girl.*

Ellis asked me to call him the next time a picture was coming in. I did a few days later, though the picture was not nearly as good as it was that first night. His large write-up appeared in July.

Springdalia
By Bob Sanders

BRUCE VAUGHAN JR. is really knocking them over with his television set, the only one in these parts so far as we know. . . . He reported yesterday he had picked up Pittsburgh, Pa.; Memphis, Tenn.; Washington, D. C.; San Francisco; and others. . . . Ordinarily a set is not supposed to pick up a program over a distance of 100 miles, but BRUCE says the atmospheric conditions at the present time are responsible. . . . We gotta get over and see that thing.

Bryan (W. J. B.) Work called on the phone. "I want to buy the first TV sold in Springdale," he said. I was glad to oblige. I installed an antenna on top of his house on Highway 68 West and delivered a 10-inch TV to his home. Reception was marginal at best.

Other early purchasers were Dr. Friedman Sisco, Vern Backus, and Bob Sanders. Within months we were selling several sets a week. Television had arrived in Northwest Arkansas.

CHAPTER 5

The Tale of the Peacock

*I find television very educational. Every time someone switches it
on, I go into another room and read a good book.*

GROUCHO MARX (1890–1977)
AMERICAN COMEDIAN

Atop a rusty iron pipe, leaning inward since its assault by a 1933 Ford sedan, the
faded street signs read "Holcomb Street" and "Emma Avenue."
A gentle south breeze, welcome after another hot August night, blows down
Holcomb Street past the First Baptist Church and continues northward between our
only fire station and the Springdale Motor Company. Reaching Emma, the cool wind
turns westward. Now a whirlwind, it swirls in a counterclockwise direction, a miniature
tornado filled with last night's refuse. Candy wrappers, paper napkins smeared with
yellow mustard and red lipstick, receipts from the Arkansas Brokerage Company and
Lichlyter's Department Store, along with scraps of ice cream cones from the Ellis Ice
Cream Parlor become airborne. The little whirlwind stops as suddenly as it started.
Tumbling downward, the trash comes to rest in front of the Arkansas Western Gas
Company at the corner of Holcomb and Emma. Such was the aerodynamics of the
busy intersection. All trash ended up in the same spot, regardless of wind direction. It
still does today.

Overhead, hundreds of stars pricked brilliant holes of light through the blue-black
canopy of summer darkness. The eastern sky, though dark, seemed eagerly awaiting
the first tints of red. It was 4:35 A.M., August 12, 1950.
I stopped my old '41 Chevrolet pickup briefly at the Holcomb-Emma intersection.
Louis Lichlyter had a nice tweed sports jacket in the window. I must stop by later in
the day and take a look at it. I turned right on Emma, made a "U" turn at the railroad
tracks, drove one block back west, and parked in front of my radio shop. Glancing at
the marquee of the Concord theater across the street, I noticed the mid-week movie
was John Ford's latest western, *Rio Grande,* with John Wayne and Maureen O'Hara. I
made a mental note to be sure to see the movie.
Yesterday, only minutes before closing time, Jones Truck Lines had delivered my

new Hickok test equipment. I helped Lester Schmidt unload the freight. It had been a long day; unpacking and installing the equipment could wait until morning.

Anxious to get a look at my new gear I found sleep difficult. Fully awake, I glanced at the luminous hands of my wrist watch. It was a few minutes till 4:00 A.M. I might as well be doing something constructive, I reasoned. By 4:30 I was dressed and ready for work. My first cup of coffee could wait. I decided to leave the house quietly and let Mary sleep another three hours. There was always a pot of black coffee on the little cast-iron gas stove in my shop.

I unlocked the large wooden door of the old building, snapped on the two ceiling lights, and stepped inside. The walnut-stained shelves in the corner, formerly used for a display of wine and bourbon when the building was occupied by Carl Hewitt's Liquor Store, are now filled with small AC-DC radios. The red, green, blue, white, and ever popular walnut-finished cabinets make a pleasing display. Along the east wall is my total TV stock: a small 12-inch Motorola table TV, a radio-phonograph-TV combination by Admiral, and one of the new 14-inch Philco consoles.

As I unpacked my new test equipment in the early morning hours, my mind filled with thoughts and plans for the future. There were so many changes in store for the electronics industry, and for the city of Springdale, that the thought boggled my mind.

Little did I realize, that morning in 1950, just how fast the changes were going to occur. Within the next three years demand for TV sets and antennas would often outrun my ability to supply.

TV screen sizes had been slowly increasing as technology overcame problem after problem. Average-priced sets ($200 to $500) now came with 12- or 14-inch picture tubes; some of the more expensive sets had the newly introduced "giant" 16-inch screen. Talk was that very soon larger tubes would be common, possibly as large as 21 inches.

I no longer had a monopoly on television in Springdale. It seemed everyone thought there was big money to be had in this new field. Rather expensive and elaborate outside antennas were required at the time, thus increasing the profit potential of each TV sale. The TV cable was still some years in the future.

CURTIS HORNOR (SEPTEMBER 1993)

. . . A rather interesting little story relating to TV in our area occurred in 1954 just after I sold my tire business. I was walking down Emma one day and happened to meet Roy Bowman. Roy was the manager for KBRS at the time. He knew I had sold out my Goodyear tire business and was not doing anything. We visited for a few minutes, and Roy asked me to go to work for him.*

"What would I be doing?" I asked.

"Well, the company (Don Reynolds) has a franchise for a TV cable here in Springdale," replied Roy. "We would like for you to do something with it."

"What on earth is a TV cable?" I asked.

Armistice Day parade marching westward on Emma shortly before 1920. Notice horse drawn vehicles mixed in with cars. Courtesy Washington County Historical Society.

Emma Avenue looking west from railroad crossing, 1921. Note "Drive Slow" sign planted firmly in the center of Emma. Walter Jones/Late Chevrolet building is first building on right. Courtesy Guy Howard.

Completed in 1922, Frisco's brick depot featured "white" and "colored" waiting rooms and drinking fountains. The "white" waiting room was heated by a coal-burning stove. Courtesy Howard Clark.

The Presbyterian Church on Spring Street served as city hall and jail for many years. The Little home is at right; a dry cleaning shop is at left. Courtesy Phillip Steele/Freddie Fink Collection.

Kennan's Jewelry Store decorated for Christmas. This was one of the first stores in Springdale to stock phonographs and phonograph records. I remember visiting this store with my mother about 1927. She was looking for a record by a new recording star named Jimmy Rodgers (1897–1933). Courtesy *The Springdale News.*

Penrod's Cafe, 1920s. Courtesy Howard Clark.

The Famous Hardware before its move from the corner of Mill Street and Emma Avenue. The same fixtures were in use until it closed in the 1980s. Courtesy The Famous Hardware Company.

Penrod's Cafe, 1935. Joe Steele sits at front table (left); "Doogie" DeWese rests arms on counter; entrance to pool room is through arched doorway at rear. Courtesy Ralph Crumpacker.

Emma Avenue, 1930s. A hand-operated pump is at Bransdall Gas and Bus Station (right). At left, a group watches a daredevil photographer on a stepladder shooting this photo. Courtesy The Famous Hardware Company.

Emma Avenue, ca. 1939–45. Courtesy Roy Nixon.

Strawberry market on Emma Avenue, 1930s. A Model A pickup is at left; berry crates are stacked in front of Jeff Brown's office at right. Courtesy The Famous Hardware Company.

Strawberry market on Emma Avenue, viewed from Pioneer Lumber Company, looking east, 1939. Temporary buyer's office is at lower right. Courtesy J. L. Charleton.

Bryan Work with his American Eaglet after it was rebuilt by Bob Boyle. It was the first locally owned plane based in Springdale. Work's little sheet-metal hangar (background) was at northeast corner of present rodeo grounds. Courtesy Bryan Work.

Joyce's Drug Store. Chris Wood (left), Mrs. Clay Carter, Clay Carter, and Charles McKinney. Courtesy Mrs. Charles McKinney.

Located at the Emma Avenue/Highway 71 intersection, this service station was built in the 1920s, primarily to service Johnson and Steele trucks and cars. It became popular because of its skilled mechanics. Courtesy Springdale Chamber of Commerce.

Jamie Coleman (center) introduced the "floor sale" to Springdale. The clerk at right is Gene Harper. Courtesy Springdale Chamber of Commerce.

Emma Avenue and Main Street intersection. This photo by Charles Bickford was very useful in placing businesses in the index to this book. Courtesy Springdale Chamber of Commerce.

Concord Theater fire, 1943. The fire spread to the Pioneer Lumber Company, but was quickly brought under control. A "Hopalong Cassidy" movie was playing at the Concord. The Opera House is at right. Courtesy Howard Clark.

The Springdale Migratory Labor Camp, 1944. When the harvest seasons ended, the canvas tops were removed from the huts until needed for the next year. The large building served social needs of the camp. Dr. Stanley Applegate had his first office in Springdale in this camp. Courtesy Howard Clark.

Post-war parade marching eastward on Emma Avenue, date unknown. Note that the First National Bank had not yet started expanding westward. The first expansion would take in the Western Auto Store. Later expansions would take in all buildings on the left up to, and including, the Lichlyter building. Courtesy *The Springdale News*.

The big snowstorm of 1946 brought business to a standstill in downtown Springdale. It was just as well because many merchants were on top of their buildings shoveling snow off the roofs to keep them from caving in. The entire marquee of the Concord Theater ended up on the sidewalk due to snow and ice load. Courtesy Bobbie Lynch/Richard Lynch, photographer.

John Late takes a last look at his "Case Room" before demolition of the building. It was the first home of Bruce's Electric Shop in 1946. Courtesy *The Springdale News*/Charles Bickford, photographer.

Bruce Vaughan shows off his new Hickok test equipment (purchased in 1948) at his shop, located in part of the old Arcade Hotel. The hotel was once owned by his grandfather, C. I. Vaughan.

Parade circa 1949. Courtesy *The Springdale News*.

Coger Drug Store. (rear, left to right) A. C. Coger, Mrs. Coger, and Clifford Samuel; unidentified clerk at counter. Courtesy Howard Clark.

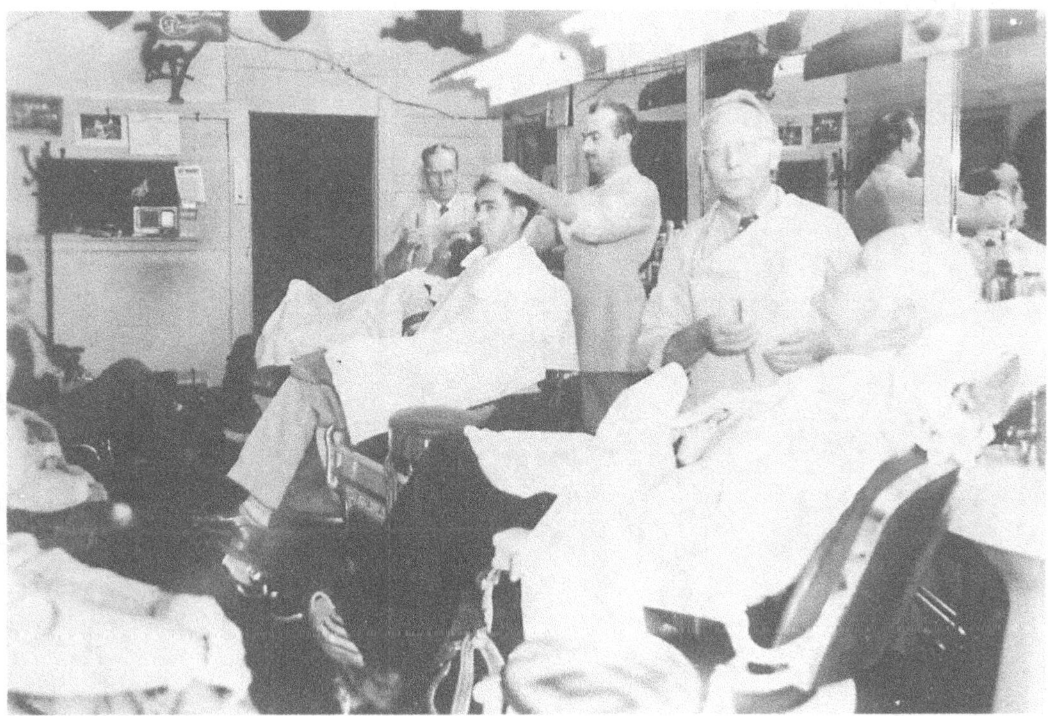

Palace Barber Shop, ca. 1950. Sam Bryant stands at back chair; Johnny Meeker (center chair) is cutting Dale Sigmon's hair; Bruce Vaughan, Sr. (front chair) shaves John Late. Bruce worked for John Late from 1938 until 1955. The only time Bruce barbered was after he and John had quarreled. John's way of showing that there were no hard feelings was to let Bruce shave him. As soon as the two had settled their differences, Bruce would return to his regular job. Courtesy John Meeker.

Early 1950s photo by Ray Watson. Springdale Savings and Loan occupies newly remodeled Farmers and Merchants Bank building between Wilson's and Coleman Shoe Store. Courtesy Ray Watson.

Howard Clark, a businessman with an engineering background, made this photo when he was drawing plans for the renovation of the old Pioneer Lumber building. Courtesy Howard Clark.

Pioneer Hardware building after the remodeling of the old Pioneer Lumber building (see previous photo). Courtesy Howard Clark.

The Pioneer Lumber and Hardware Company (left) was liquidated in the summer of 1955 (note closed door of lumber shed). This photo was probably made shortly after the store ceased operation. Courtesy Roy Nixon.

A caravan of rodeo boosters return to Springdale, after a long, hot trip to surrounding towns, ca. 1957. Such caravans contributed to the rapid growth of the rodeo crowds in the 1950s. Courtesy Bobbie Byars Lynch.

The East Side Recreation Parlor (once occupied by Masoner's Grocery) was photographed on a rainy, stormy night, 1959. Bruce Vaughan, photographer.

Emma Avenue, prior to Urban Renewal Project, early 1950s. Courtesy Springdale Chamber of Commerce.

Governor Orval Faubus (right) visits with Espen and Lois Walters in front of the Palace Barber Shop, ca. 1964. Courtesy *The Springdale News*/Charles Bickford, photographer.

The exodus of businesses from Emma Avenue to Highway 71 began in the late 1950s. Some who moved were: Bruce's Radio & TV, Harp's Grocery, Loyd's Shoe Shop, Clark and Eoff Furniture, and Hewitt's Liquor Store. 1965. Courtesy *The Springdale News*/Charles Bickford, photographer.

The corner of Spring Street and Emma Avenue was popular with loafers and curbside preachers, who sometimes attracted heckling and catcalls. 1965. Courtesy *The Springdale News*/Charles Bickford, photographer.

Downtown merchants and employees were encouraged to dress in western attire to promote the annual Rodeo of the Ozarks. Failure to do so meant being sent to "jail." Freedom could be obtained by paying a fine or escaping through a well-filled tank of water, emerging free, but wet. Those identified are: 1) Roy McCamey, 2) Russell Harrison, 3) Sandy Boone, 4) Wayne High, 5) Elmer Johnson, 6) Jim Reis, 7) Pete Jones, 8) Tommy Haseloff, 9) Sonny Henson, 10) Police Chief Wayne Hyden. Bruce Vaughan, photographer.

Jeff Brown's Feed Mill. Bruce Vaughan, photographer.

Tyson' Feed Mill. Bruce Vaughan, photographer.

Use of a long telephoto lens enabled photographer Charles Bickford to capture almost the entire Emma Avenue business district, as it existed in May of 1967. Courtesy *The Springdale News*/Charles Bickford, photographer.

Many of Emma Avenue's old buildings were replaced by modern ones during the Urban Renewal Project. San Jose Manor now stands behind the sign at right. 1967. Courtesy *The Springdale News*/Charles Bickford, photographer.

This 1968 photo shows rather light traffic on Emma Avenue. The shadows under the cars indicate it was probably made at the noon hour. Courtesy *The Springdale News*/Charles Bickford, photographer.

This church building served as our City Hall and Jail for many years. It was demolished in 1967 when major changes were made to our downtown area. Courtesy *The Springdale News*/Charles Bickford, photographer.

Paving Main Street circa 1969. Jerry Biazo snapped this picture when he was a photographer for the *News*. Courtesy *The Springdale News*/Jerry Biazo, photographer.

Mayor Park Phillips (right) and Bob Irons, superintendent of Johnson-Egli Company, who did the Spring Creek channelization, inspect progress on the Urban Renewal Project (south of Emma, looking north). 1973. Courtesy *The Springdale News*/Charles Bickford, photographer.

San Jose Manor (beyond Wilson's) had been completed when this photo was made. Work was still in progress behind fences on both sides of Emma Avenue. 1973. Courtesy *The Springdale News*/Charles Bickford, photographer.

James Carpenter (left) and Bruce Vaughan pause in the shade at the ground-breaking ceremony for the new Shiloh Museum of Ozark History building, May 11, 1990. Both men were in the radio business long before the arrival of television. Their association was one of cooperation and friendly competition, as they shared knowledge and information. Courtesy *The Morning News*/Charles Bickford, photographer.

"I don't have the slightest idea," answered Roy, "but if I understand it correctly, they put up a big TV antenna somewhere, then run wires from it to homes and business buildings in town."

*B. J. Hainbach owned the Hudson auto dealership (#9A) after WWII and operated it for several years. This is the building occupied in the early 1950s by Curtis Hornor's Goodyear store. During the '30s it was the Lindley Motor Company (Lester Lindley, Dodge and Plymouth dealer).

My reply was, "And they charge money for that!"
"Yes, that is the general idea," replied Roy.
"Why would anyone pay for something they can get for free?" I asked.
"I have no idea," answered Roy.
We discussed the whole idea for a few more minutes and agreed that the entire concept was impractical.
They sold the franchise a short time later to the Texas Cable Association. You can see how Roy and I miscalculated the concept of TV cable.

It is easy to understand why Curtis was reluctant to embark on a new career based on the TV cable concept.

Sometime around 1950 I sold Joe Steele a 100-foot tower and a 16-inch TV set. That was when Joe lived up on West Emma in the large two-story house. Reception left a lot to be desired, even with the best antenna available.

Joe called me one Sunday and asked me to come by his house. He greeted me at the door, invited me in, and then turned on the TV. It was a snowy picture, subject to complete fade-outs occasionally.

"Is there anything we can do to improve my reception?" Mr. Steele wanted to know.

"I don't know of a thing we can do that we have not already done," I replied.

Joe picked up a section of the Sunday paper, pointed to a column, and handed it to me. "Read this," he said.

It was a story about how some towns in deep fringe areas were getting better TV reception by installing large antenna arrays as high as possible, usually on top of a nearby mountain, and running cables to homes in the town. Naturally, there was a monthly charge for the service.

I had read of the concept in various technical publications. "Joe, that involves a lot of money," I said. "There is the problem of securing right-of-way for the lines, maintaining poles, providing amplifiers every few hundred feet because of loss in the coaxial cable, and maintaining personnel and vehicles. The cost would run into more money than I will ever see."

"I'll finance the project if you will manage the business," replied Joe. "Look it over, put a pencil to it, and get back to me. I think it might be the coming thing for towns like ours."

The logical place for the antenna was East Mountain. I measured the distance from there to the west end of Emma. Then I tried to estimate the cost to install the tower and antennas, along with the associated cables and equipment. It was obvious the antenna system was a very small part of the overall cost. The real cost was in getting the signal into the homes.

I counted homes and measured distances on other streets. I guessed we would eventually get 80% of TV owners to subscribe to our service. A few days later I took the figures to Mr. Steele.

"I'm sorry, but by my estimate there is no way in the world that a TV cable system here in Springdale will ever be practical," I said.

BILL BAILEY (MARCH 1994)

The TV Cable Company got its start when our Texas-based parent company bought the cable franchise from Don Reynolds.

Some of our Texas people came up and made an initial survey. They were not too optimistic. It seemed almost every house in Springdale had a good TV antenna. We were not sure they would pay us more money to see TV, even though we could deliver a much better picture.

I was one of the first employees of the new company. My job was climbing poles and stringing coaxial cable.

1958 was our first year of operation. The last day of 1958 we worked from daylight to dark, hooking up new subscribers. Everyone wanted to watch the New Year's football games. Before dark we hooked up our 200th subscriber; it was quite a thrill.

Our monthly charge was $4.75. We had a hook-up charge, but often accepted the new subscriber's TV antenna as our initial payment.

Today we have 15,000 subscribers. We are too busy trying to keep up with demand to make projections. There are many new things in store for TV cable viewers. Some of the newer ideas stagger the mind.

In the near future it is probable that a subscriber can, for a modest charge, order up a movie for instant viewing. He will have over 5,000 different titles to choose from.

"It would seem that you, Roy Bowman, and I all underestimated the potential of TV cable," I said. "Curtis, what can you tell me about the early days of radio stations here in Northwest Arkansas?"

CURTIS HORNOR

Even though I was wrong about the cable, I went to work for KBRS on July 1, 1958.

Incidentally, the tower used by the TV cable out on East Mountain is the top half of the KBRS tower.

> *When Mr. Reynolds put the station (KBRS) on the air in 1949, he brought the tower up from Fort Smith. It was somewhere around 350 feet tall. I don't know whether it was regulations or because of engineering purposes, but the decision was made to make the KBRS antenna 156 feet tall. The balance of the antenna was sold to the TV cable people. The tower is still in use out there on East Mountain.*

"What happened to the old KBRS station, Curtis?" I asked. "Was it sold as a station and moved, or did they just piecemeal the equipment out?"

> *Actually, I retired in 1985, and they called me back to work twice after that. They couldn't keep a manager. Finally, in the early '80s, AM radio went into a slide as far as revenue was concerned. The slide rapidly became a nose dive. AM, quite simply, could not compete with FM radio. I read the handwriting on the wall and decided it was a good time for me to retire. It was the best decision I ever made, because AM radio more or less went to pot after that.*
>
> *They finally sold the station in either '88 or '89; very shortly, the buyer went bankrupt. The Donrey Media Group had to take the station back. They sold it to radio station KJEM in 1992. They sold everything, including the real estate.*

The early years of TV were full of uncertainty. There was talk of running underground coaxial cables throughout the United States, connecting every TV station to a central point, thus making national programming a reality. This impractical solution was soon replaced by a plan to use microwave towers, rather than coaxial cable.

In the early 1950s, video tape recording remained a dream. A few working models could be found in laboratories, but the equipment was large, heavy, expensive, and produced images of poor quality. The old crooner himself, Bing Crosby, invested a fortune in a company attempting to develop practical video tape recorders for commercial use. No one dared to hope that they might sometime be available for home use.

Stations had but two choices of program material: shows on standard movie film or live shows produced in the studio. Such things as sporting events, political conventions, and news events, unless they occurred within the range of the local TV station, could not be covered "live." They had to be filmed by a movie crew, the film developed and edited, then flown by air to TV stations throughout the country.

And what of color TV? The Federal Communications Commission (FCC) had not decided which system of color television to adopt as our standard. NBC was sure it had the answer in the three-gun color tube with electronic scanning. CBS was pushing their mechanical system, because it was "fully compatible" with every black and white TV, old or new. The CBS system used a motor-driven, three-color disc placed in front of any monochrome TV. A similar disc was placed in front of the studio camera. In theory, if you could get both discs revolving at the same speed, the monochrome picture would appear in color. I shudder to think what the results might have been if the FCC had gone with the CBS system.

Other Springdale merchants stocking TV sets included: Stanley Watson (Watson Tire and Supply), Lawrence Layman (East Side Grocery), Eddie and Paul Cummings (The Famous Hardware Company), Cecil Brown (Oklahoma Tire and Supply), Dick Kinmouth (Western Auto), and Jim Carpenter (Jim's Radio). Howard Clark and Dupree Deaver of the Clark-Deaver Hardware Company remained firm in their decision not to sell television until it became more dependable. Their decision was difficult to keep; pressure from the RCA distributor, anxious to increase sales, was constantly increasing.

Surprisingly, we had very few dissatisfied customers, though those early years of television were difficult for both the dealers and customers. It was a new adventure, considered by most as a learning experience.

Little did we dream the small "Sputnik" satellite launched by the Russians on October 4, 1957, would solve many problems confronting the TV industry. No longer was there talk of the excessively expensive and time consuming project of thousands of miles of underground coaxial cable and installation of hundreds of microwave towers. Satellites costing a few million dollars could do the job that would have cost billions— even if they were in the realm of possibility.

America was intoxicated with victories in Europe and the Pacific. After the unexpected and abrupt end of WWII (brought about by a mysterious new weapon, the atomic bomb), people were ready to believe anything was possible—and likely to happen. These were the wonderful post-war years for which we had fought and sacrificed.

Every morning we Americans scanned the papers to see what new wonders would come next. After all, we were living in the Atomic Age. It was the age of Lustron Homes, Tucker and Kaiser automobiles, jet-powered airplanes, television, cinemascope, penicillin, aerosol cans, FM, TV, and women's skirts below the knees, known in fashion circles as "The New Look."

About 1948, Webster-Chicago introduced the wire recorder, a machine by which the user could record voice or music on a thin strand of wire. A small spool about three inches in diameter held hundreds of feet of the recording wire. The fidelity of recorded music was marginal at best—if you could keep from breaking the wire and ending up with a tangled mess. Many electronic trade magazines writers were predicting the possibility of home recorders that would actually record in stereo.

In the late 1940s "flying saucer" stories were as common as fleas at a houn' dog convention. Fort Smith had a race track named the "Flying Saucer Speedway," and there were "flying saucer" cafes located in most cities of any size. Newspapers, the radio, and national news magazines carried numerous stories of unexplained flying objects.

One morning, over coffee at Penrod's, Howard "Nub" Clark and I decided we could create some real excitement along Emma Avenue if we could launch some flying saucers and have them pass over downtown Springdale. During the coming days many ideas were considered, then discarded. Some airborne objects were too expensive, some totally impractical, and some, like tissue paper hot-air balloons, far too dangerous. We only wanted to cause some excitement, not burn down the town. A classified ad in *Popular Mechanics* solved our problem.

Howard and I split the cost and ordered three large weather balloons. We decided to solicit the help of Vol Lester (then manager of the Springdale office of the Arkansas Western Gas Company—later, Judge Lester). We needed Vol. He could fill the balloons with natural gas at the substation on the corner of Emma and West End Street. There was plenty of pressure there. The three of us met every morning at Penrod's to polish our plans for the hoax. At last, the three weather balloons arrived.

We watched the weather carefully. Ideal conditions required a southwesterly wind, no more than three or four miles per hour, and a clear sky. It was decided by the three of us that late afternoon would be the ideal time to launch our "saucers." Our plan was to inflate the balloons at the substation, tie them to my truck, and drive to a position near the present St. Raphael's Catholic Church. Please keep in mind—this area was not heavily populated at that time. When the long awaited day arrived, it was like a drive in the country.

Once at our launch site, we sprayed the balloons with silver paint and attached enough weight (rocks) to make sure they passed over town at an altitude of less than one thousand feet. Our theory was that the sun would reflect off the balloons, making them seem to shimmer in the bright light at this low altitude. For dramatic effect we wanted the ground in deep shade.

Our first balloon did not have enough weight attached. It gained altitude quickly, within seconds becoming virtually indiscernible in the late afternoon sky. We were more careful with the two remaining. Enough weight was attached so that they gained barely enough altitude to clear the light and telephone wires along the south side of Highway 68. We launched one; then thirty seconds later the second followed.

As balloon number two cleared the power lines, we jumped in my truck and hurried to town. I parked in front of the OTASCO store. The three of us walked slowly down the street and took our positions on the curb in front of Penrod's. The balloons were moving slower than we expected.

At last, the two brilliant orbs came into view. To our disappointment no one looked skyward. Vol, Nub, and I stood on the curb gazing upward, pointing to the "saucers." Time was running out; we realized our money and efforts were about to pass over Springdale completely unnoticed, unless we acted quickly.

A young boy selling *Grit* papers came out of the Palace Barber Shop. I turned to him, then pointed at the sky, "What in the world do you think those things are?" I asked.

"Flying saucers! Flying saucers!" he yelled. Then he ran into Penrod's. "There are a couple of flying saucers goin' over!" yelled the young man. "Come quick! Flying saucers!"

People rushed outside. Everyone, including all the kitchen help, lined the sidewalk and pointed upward. Drivers noticed the commotion and stopped where they were, jumping from their vehicles to peer at the strange sight.

Kennedy Deaver was among those along the curb. "I was in the Navy. I am sure those are nothing but weather balloons," he said. No one wanted to hear a logical explanation . . . it was more thrilling to believe they were really "flying saucers."

Soon the two balloons were out of sight, drifting to the northeast.

It was several years before Howard and I confessed that we were the instigators of the hoax. By then, most people had forgotten Springdale's only "Brief Encounter."

> *A man is his own easiest dupe, for what he wishes to be true, he generally believes to be true.*
>
> DEMOSTHENES (C. 384–322 BC)
> GREEK POLITICIAN

The Palace Barber Shop, like Penrod's, was a favorite hang-out. Carl Hewitt, one of the regulars, came by every morning for a shave, often staying around to visit. Carl loved to play pranks on his friends. Howard Ewalt was often on the receiving end of Carl's jokes. The stories that follow were told to me by barbers who worked in the Palace.

Howard was always well-dressed and extremely conscious of his appearance. He was also sensitive to opinions of others. Carl used this trait to the amusement of the barber shop bunch.

One morning Carl had just stepped down out of the barber chair, when he looked across the street and saw Howard emerge from Wilson's wearing a new hat. Autry must have sold him the best hat in the house; it looked expensive and was the latest style. Howard started across the street to the barber shop.

Quickly, Carl turned to the crowd and said, "Look at Howard! He has a brand new hat. When he comes in, I want everyone to glance at the hat, then look away and grin—not too much, don't over do it. I'll take care of the rest."

Howard opened the door and entered. Everyone spoke as he made his way to the back of the shop to hang up his new hat. When he turned around, everyone avoided eye contact with him. Some were grinning; others could best be described as snickering.

"Howard, I hate to say anything, but if I was you, I'd buy a new hat," said Carl. "You can afford it, and that style went out years ago. Being in your business (insurance), I'd think it would pay to wear a current style. A fellow has got to be careful of his appearance."

Howard blushed a little, but said nothing. After his shave, he put on the new hat and left the shop. Carl watched him from the window. "I'll bet you a ten dollar bill he goes home and puts that hat in the closet. He'll never wear it again."

Mr. Ewalt walked directly to his new Buick, then drove up Spring Street toward his home. Ten minutes later he returned, parked in front of his office, and stepped out of his car, wearing a different hat.

"I knew I could upset him," said Carl. "Remember when he bought that expensive wrist watch from Hoyt Perry? I told him everyone up and down Emma was laughing, because the model he bought was giving a lot of trouble."

He put his old watch back on and never wore the new one again.

One cold, snowy winter day, Carl and some of the fellows in the Palace were standing in the front window watching the heavy snowfall. A young boy, twelve years old or so, walked by the barber shop. He was wearing a tattered summer shirt and worn canvas shoes. It was obvious the kid was cold and wet. Without a word, Carl stepped outside, walked up to the kid, and started talking. Soon, the two of them walked across the street and stepped into Wilson's Department Store.

Twenty minutes later Carl and the boy stepped out of Wilson's store. The kid had on new clothes from head to foot, including a nice warm coat. Carl returned to the barber shop. No one mentioned the incident; Carl would have been embarrassed if they had.

On another occasion Carl played a joke on the kid that sold *Grit* newspapers. This young fellow started to work on the sidewalks of Emma early in the morning and was on the street all day selling his papers. He never seemed to tire of the heavy bag of papers he carried. His sales method never varied, whether on the street or in a public building. He stepped directly in front each person, and while looking directly into their eyes, he would say, "Do you wanna buy a *Grit?*" If the answer was negative, and it usually was, he advanced to the next person, again asking, "Do you wanna buy a *Grit?*" During rush hours in Penrod's it could take the better part of an hour to make sure everyone was given the opportunity to buy a paper.

One day Carl was in the barber shop when they saw the kid approaching. "Tell you what," said Carl. "Let's give that kid the surprise of his life. I want every one of you to buy a paper this time."

The paper boy stepped in front of Carl and said, "Do you wanna buy a *Grit?*"

"Yes, I do," answered Carl, handing the boy the money.

Sam Bryant was next; he also bought a paper—then Dan Hannah, Raymond Ford, and a few waiting for a haircut.

After selling a dozen papers or so, the kid stopped short. "Oh, no, you don't," he said. "I know what you are up to. You are trying to put me out of business."

With that he left the barber shop and returned to Emma. "Wanna buy a *Grit?*" he asked the next man passing by.

The Palace Barber Shop was a center of practical jokes. One favorite joke was to whittle a potato into the shape of a piece of shaving soap, then slip it in a barber's shaving mug. Everyone would sit around waiting for someone to get in the barber's chair and ask for a shave.

The barber would clip a apron on his customer, lean him back in the chair, and pick up his shaving mug. With his brush he would start whipping the "soap," trying to work up a thick lather. Even though the joke was old, it was always good for a laugh seeing the expression on the barber's face when he was unable to get the potato to lather. Customers enjoyed the joke and never became irritated at the delay.

On another occasion some of the fellows talked one of their out of town friends into helping with a joke. They found some old clothes which they covered with dirt, grime, and grease. Then they took two pounds of Limburger and rubbed into the clothing. The friend put on the stinking clothes.

Sam Bryant was to be the victim of their joke. One by one, the fellows ambled into the barber shop until there was standing room only. Then the "smelly one" came into the shop. He waited patiently for his turn in Sam's chair. As previously arranged, no one seemed to notice the odor but Sam. When the stinking stranger got into Sam's chair, he said, "Give me the works . . . a shave, haircut, and shampoo."

Sam looked a little pale, but endured the ordeal. As soon as he had the man's face covered with a hot towel, Sam grabbed his bottle of lilac water and started spraying the area around the chair. That is when the laughter started . . .

I don't know who was more relieved, Sam or the poor man who wore the Limburger-covered clothing. He headed directly for the shower room.

Penrod's Cafe, without question, was one of Springdale's most loved institutions. Established soon after World War I by Jack and Henry Penrod, it served the citizens of Springdale for over thirty years. The founders were husband and wife. Henry was the wife's name. Even when the front of the fine old restaurant was defaced with knotty pine and renamed The Hitchin' Post, it remained Penrod's in the hearts of Springdale's citizens.

The restaurant opened before 7:00 A.M. and remained open until well after 9:00 P.M. The breakfast rush was over by 9:00. Then tables and booths filled quickly with business men and workers from the downtown area. The Wurlitzer juke box and pin ball machines became quiet for a while, as conversation, and sometimes heated arguments, dominated the dining room. Sports and politics were favored topics, but often a group surrounding a table might be found discussing automobiles, aviation, religion, or even the latest movie with Betty Grable or Lana Turner, then playing at the Concord.

Dean Allen and Robert Spencer seemed to thoroughly enjoy their heated arguments —and they occurred daily. Republican versus Democrat, liberal versus conservative—it was better than *Firing Line* on TV. They remained the best of friends, though at times it seemed sure they would resort to violence before leaving the restaurant.

At other tables, caffeine quarterbacks and black coffee coaches rehashed last Saturday's Razorback game. There was not a man present who could not give game-winning advice to both the coach and players.

Most of the coffee crowd returned to work by 10:00 A.M., though a few lingered here and there, trying to find a quitting place for their topic of discussion.

The "Plate Lunch" crowd started arriving almost as soon as the coffee drinkers left. In 1946, a plate lunch cost from forty to sixty cents. A steak and French fries would set you back seventy-five cents. Coffee and cokes went from five to ten cents very soon after the war. Sandwiches cost from fifteen cents to a quarter.

Afternoons, there was a short lull in business from 2:00 to 2:30 P.M. From 2:30 till

3:15 downtown business personnel came in for a afternoon break; they knew it was then or never. As soon as school turned out at 3:15, there was standing room only.

The noise level increased when the high school crowd arrived. Bubbles arose in a never-ending stream through the colored plastic tubing of the Wurlitzer juke box. Red, blue, and yellow lights were an integral part of the polished mahogany cabinet of this shrine to swing. The latest Benny Goodman or Tommy Dorsey hits were ground out from 78 RPM records, scratchy from innumerable playings. Through the wail of saxophones and the blare of trumpets could be heard the chatter of many teenage voices in animated conversation, often punctuated with loud bursts of laughter. For two hours each day there were hamburgers in paradise.

The school crowd started drifting out, heading for home, about 5:00. Their vacated tables and booths were occupied immediately by the dinner crowd. Salesmen, couples on a date, families having a meal out, business men entertaining prospects—everyone ate at Penrod's. There was very little slow-up in business until after 9:30 P.M.

Two pool tables in the back room were always in use, it seemed. Sometimes you had to wait more than an hour to get one of the tables.

Yes, Penrod's was many things to many people. No one who grew up in Springdale during the years between 1920 and 1960 will ever forget it. Perhaps our government should consider giving tax breaks to establishments similar to Penrod's. It kept young people off the streets and out of trouble, provided a meeting place for adults, and offered companionship and entertainment for senior citizens. In addition, young people needing a job could usually find work at the restaurant. Government-sponsored programs normally accomplish much less.

I rented the former Liquor Store building from Uncle Jake Pogue's son-in-law. For some reason, he refused to sign any sort of a lease. I was reluctant to make repairs on the old structure, because I knew any month could be my last one there. I liked my upstairs neighbors—Dr. A. J. Harrison, M. D., and Dr. Leonard Smith, D. D. S. There was a lot of history hidden in the old clay brick of the little building. At one time it was a part of the old Arcade Hotel. When I was born in 1922, the Arcade was owned by my grandfather. In 1930, my dad had a restaurant in the building next door, later occupied by the Blue Castle.

Often I would be in the front of my store when Dr. Harrison returned to his office from making house calls. He approached his parking space slowly— apparently he had trouble judging distance. On rare occasions he managed to park the old Mercury coupe between the yellow lines. Climbing slowly from his car, he would reach in the back seat and retrieve his doctor's bag, hobble to the curb with it, then lower it to the sidewalk while he fished in his pocket for parking meter coins. Most times, he was so tired he had to lean on the parking meter for a brief rest before walking up the steps. It took all the energy he had to make it to his upstairs office, where several patients waited his return.

Both he and Dr. Smith gave away more medical service than they collected for. It was that time in history and that part of town.

In 1948, I had a flare-up with my appendix. Dr. Friedman Sisco was my doctor. He recommended surgery. The only hospital in the area was the old Washington County Hospital in Fayetteville. The hospital looked like a movie set from Hemingway's *For Whom the Bell Tolls*. There was no such thing as a maternity wing or a recovery room. The old hospital preferred "wards"—large rooms that housed a dozen or more patients at a time. Under such circumstances the patient lost his dignity, his modesty, and whatever organs the attending doctor chose to remove.

I was one of the lucky patients. I was wheeled directly from surgery to a room on the second floor, next to a maternity patient.

Dr. Harrison was attending the unfortunate lady. She was about thirty-five years old, in poor health, had seven or eight children, and a worthless husband. She was having a rough delivery. While waiting for the child to enter this world of strife and trouble, Dr. Harrison rested in the only doctors' lounge available, the worn wooden steps outside her room. Her labor pains were coming about every sixty seconds. Every time she had a labor pain, she would let out a loud moan that could be heard throughout the upper floor.

Dr. A. J. Harrison, sitting on the steps with his head in his hands, suffered right along with his patient. After each moan he would shake his head and say, "That pore woman . . . that pore woman."

Sixty seconds later, after her next wail of pain, he would say with a vengeance, "That son of a bitch . . . that son of a bitch."

He was consistent . . . he alternated from "poor woman" to "son of a bitch," until the woman delivered a child. I think both terms were appropriate.

Dr. Harrison lived next door to Dr. Friedman Sisco out on North Mill Street. The Siscos had a 12-inch TV, a present to her grandsons, Charles and Kenneth, from Mrs. C. P. Sisco.

Dr. Harrison decided his family might enjoy TV, especially his daughter Mabel, a polio victim, who was partially disabled. Mabel was a music teacher and lived with her parents.

I delivered the latest 16-inch set to the Harrisons and gave every member of the household a lengthy lesson in the operation of this new miracle.

Two days later, I received a frantic phone call from Mabel. "Come out here quick! I just turned my set on, and it is making a funny noise."

"What, exactly, is your set doing?" I asked.

"There is a round circle on the screen. There are a lot of little marks on it, and the set is going WHEEEEEEEEEEEE."

I glanced at my watch. It was too early for the Tulsa station to be on the air. I explained that, when stations were not on the air, they often ran a test pattern for adjustment of both the station and TV sets in the field.

No amount of talk could convince Mabel that her set was not going to explode.

I made a fast trip to Dr. Harrison's home. Once I looked at the set and showed Mabel how we used the pattern to set linearity adjustments, she was satisfied.

HAZEL VAUGHAN (AGE 93, MARCH 1994)

Dr. A. J. Harrison lived across the road from us at Spring Valley. I don't know what year he moved there, but it was around the turn of the century.

Dr. Harrison's wife was named Kitty. They had two girls—Mabel, a little younger than me, and Mamie, a little older. Mabel became sick with polio when she was about six years old. We didn't know it was contagious. Mamie and I entertained her by playing with dolls on her bed.

Every two weeks or so, Dr. Crutcher, the dentist, came out to Spring Valley to see patients. He drove his horse and buggy, of course, and tied his horse up in front of our house. Sometimes, he would bring me a apple to eat.

Dr. Crutcher put a big wash tub on the Harrison's front porch. Then he put a wooden rocking chair on the tub. The rockers rested on the rim of the tub. He could tilt the rocker backward to work on the patient's teeth. It made a pretty good dental chair. He threw his old bloody rags and wads of cotton into the tub. People came from all over to see the dentist.

I was about eight years old when the Harrisons moved to Lowell. I went to high school in Springdale. I stayed with Grandma Sanders. She lived on the corner of Blair and Grove. Some Fridays I went home with Mamie for the weekend. We rode the train from Springdale to Lowell. I thought it was a real vacation and looked forward to it for days. It was a big thing for me.

Lucien Parker, a Hindsville native recently moved to Springdale, bought a building just east of the Bon-Ton Cleaners. He remodeled the building and divided it into two small buildings. He found out I was unhappy with my rental arrangement and offered me a three-year lease, with a three-year option, for fifty dollars a month—only ten more than I was now paying. Though I realized it was smaller than I needed, I decided to make the move. The year was 1951.

Television sets had become larger. Now, 21-inch picture tubes were the standard size. In 1953, General Electric introduced the "Black Daylight" TV. The public was eager for anything that promised a better picture. The new GEs did seem to help reduce the snowy appearance of pictures in deep fringe areas*, such as Springdale. Actually,

---

* Fringe area is a term seldom heard today. Back in the late 1940s and early 1950s the term was familiar to millions. A combination of low-gain tuners in TV sets, low powered transmitting stations, and low-station antenna heights limited the range of good TV reception to about 50 miles, sometimes much less, depending upon terrain. The TV sets were an instant hit. We began to place orders for ten to twenty-five sets at a time. Imagine, if you will, unloading twenty boxes, each about three feet square, trying to unpack, and displaying them in a store building only ten feet wide. It simply was not possible. I decided the time had come to start planning on a business building on Highway 71. I purchased a lot from W. C. Rogers, one block south of the Highway 68 intersection. As I had quite some time left on my lease, I made a decision to start the building in the spring. I was sure Mr. Parker would work with me on my arrangements.

the TV sets offered no miracle, just a darker screen coating, plus a dark safety glass in front of the tube. The sets did give the effect of a better picture.

RCA was talking about introducing color TV at this time. I intended to be first with color, just as I had been with black and white. I placed an order for a color set to be delivered when they became available. I was notified that the set would be delivered in the fall of '54.

The RCA people suggested that I attend a color TV school they were sponsoring at the Goldman Hotel in Fort Smith. Jim Carpenter and I made reservations for the school. As color TV was new to both of us, we thoroughly enjoyed the school.

My RCA color TV was delivered soon afterward. It used a 16-inch metal picture tube, came in a plain plywood cabinet, and cost $542.10 wholesale. The same year I bought a deluxe cab Chevrolet pickup with many extras. The truck cost me $1,425 delivered, taxes paid.

Only a few hours of color were available each week. Those few color programs were introduced by the RCA peacock spreading his multicolored tail across the TV screen. Buyers of those first color TV sets paid about forty dollars per feather to look at the peacock's tail. Was it worth the cost? I really don't know . . . it's difficult to put a price on being first. It has always cost more to lead than to follow. Perhaps those first customers did pay a big price. However, we must remember that without those first sales, the development of TV would not have progressed to the point where we can all enjoy excellent quality and low cost television, as we do today.

CHAPTER 6

The Survivors

The cowards never started,

The weak died along the way,

Only the strongest survived.

HAROLD WARP
INVENTOR

The quotation above is from a marker near the entrance to Harold Warp's Pioneer Village in Minden, Nebraska. The marker is a tribute to the hardy men and women who opened up the West. The quotation would be appropriate when talking of America's small businessmen.

Before anyone starts a new business, he must have four things: faith in himself, faith in the area, good employees, and nerve enough to risk everything on a dream. Unfortunately, most new business ventures are doomed to failure. Only the best, only the very strongest, will survive. A limited few of those starting a new business will achieve greatness—success beyond their dreams. Even those destined for prominence may find the road upward has its hazards.

RAY WATSON (SEPTEMBER 1990)

I went to work for Harvey Jones back in the twenties. I was young, but big for my years—and I was a good driver. We didn't have so many government regulations back then.

One of the "runs" I had for a time was from here to Springfield and back. It doesn't seem far now, but then the road was unpaved. They called it gravel, but it was more like mud. I remember one trip I made—I think it was in late November. I forget what I hauled up there, but my return trip was a truck load of King heaters. I'm sure you remember those cheap heating stoves. They were made of metal not much heavier than a stovepipe. I don't think the stove weighed over thirty pounds, including the cardboard box it was packed in.

Well, this was an old flat-bed truck I was driving. Of course we had no heater, and in addition the windshield was broken. It was knocked out some days before when a truck in front of me kicked up a rock—not exactly a comfortable way to travel.

We got the King heaters all loaded and tied down around four in the afternoon. I buttoned up my coat, pulled my cap down over my ears, and started home. If all went well, I could make Springdale before midnight.

Somewhere up near the state line it started snowing. I was frozen stiff, but my big worry was the heaters. If my load got wet, those cardboard boxes would start coming apart. I knew from experience that those cheap stoves rusted almost immediately if they got wet.

Jones Truck Lines was a small operation then. Harvey was just getting started and could not afford to carry a lot of insurance. As a matter of fact, I knew there was no insurance at all on the load. If I lost the load, it would cost Harvey a lot of money.

I knew that if I kept the truck moving, the wind would blow most of the snow off the boxes. When I got to Springdale, I could run the truck inside. Jones had a sheet-iron building that would house three or four trucks. If any snow was left on the load, I intended to sweep it off with a broom.

About 11:00 P.M. I headed down Emma, driving as fast as I thought I could get away with. I slowed up a little for the railroad tracks, then opened it up. When I turned off Emma into our lot, I breathed easy and headed for our warehouse. Lucky for me, the door was open.

What I forgot to figure was the height of load. I had the heaters stacked five high. The door was a bit lower. With a crash, the King heaters hit the tin building and went flying all over our lot. Harvey, worried about his truck and driver, was still in his office. When he heard the commotion, he came running out to see what had happened.

Well, we both wanted to cry when we started picking up the pieces. After a couple of hours work we realized it was not as bad as it looked. We salvaged most of the load. The loss, even though small, was still important to the new truck line. By the way, Harvey never blamed me at all. He even told me later that he appreciated my effort to save the load of heaters.

MARY SELLERS (APRIL 1994)

I started to work for Jones Truck Lines in 1934. Ray was working there then. I remember our old metal buildings, though I don't recall the incident mentioned by Ray.

When I was a kid, we lived across the road from the airport (now rodeo grounds).

Stobaugh had a little grocery store and filling station on the corner. Bryan Work's airplane hangar was just east of the store.

My brothers, Bill and Eugene, and I used to play all over that area. Once in a while Bryan would give us a ride in his airplane. I knew my parents preferred that I stay on the ground. When I got home, they would have another talk with me.

Bryan had the only plane hangared at the airport in the late twenties.

As our town grew, so did our more successful business firms. The business survivors all seemed to share certain basic traits. They made more good decisions than bad. They refused to give up when it appeared their business was failing. They understood their customers' needs and supplied those needs.

Clarkson's Mercantile is a classic example.

MORRIS CLARKSON (SEPTEMBER 1993)

Dad went into business over on the east side in 1930. He was in the hardware business down on Emma some ten years before that. Dad was a stockholder in the Washington County Hardware. L. M. Riggs was the majority stock holder. There may have been others involved that I don't know about. They built that building (#48).

The Famous was across the street on the corner of Emma and Mill (#65). Then, in the mid-thirties, The Famous moved into the Washington County building and absorbed the assets of the Washington County Hardware.

Wilson's then moved from the building on the corner of Spring and Emma (#71) into the building on the corner of Mill and Emma (#65).

Dad bought out a grocery and dry goods store from a Mr. Forbes. The building was on the corner of Graham and Emma, just east of the old East Side Hotel. Of course, the building was much smaller then. The main building was actually two buildings, each 25 feet wide (#123). Dad added a 30-foot building (#124) on the east and extended the depth of all three buildings by 25 feet. This gave us over 6,000 sq. ft.

I remember the old Lichlyter building was considered one of Springdale's larger stores. When I bought the building (#36) some twenty years ago, I was surprised to find it was only twenty-eight feet wide. Twenty feet was about the average store width before World War II.

The Lichlyter building was one of the first brick buildings in Springdale. I'm sure this was the location of The Leader. I have a lot of early photographs that bear this out. One night, shortly after World War II, the building burned. When it was built back, the upper story was eliminated, and the stairway entrance removed.

Lichlyter's alteration department was on the second floor. Some speculated that the fire started from an electric iron accidentally left on after the store closed. However, I don't know that the cause of the fire was ever confirmed.

MORRIS CLARKSON

Yes, I remember that Dr. R. T. Henry's office was located upstairs above Lichlyter's. The building west of Lichlyter's was the Southwestern Gas and Electric offices. The J. W. and L. S. Phillips insurance and real estate office (the Ozark Land Company) was over the Electric office.

> *There was another nice store downtown. It was up there where Martini's*
> *Arkansas Brokerage was located. It was called The Hub. It was directly across*
> *the street from the Washington County Hardware. I believe The Hub, or a store*
> *in the same location, was owned by Smyer—I recall the names Dot (Dorothy)*
> *and Bert (Bertha?) Smyer. Down on the corner of Mill and Emma was the Cash*
> *Dry Goods. It was owned by John Meyers.*

When I was in college, I used to play golf. I never played very well. I found it hard to dig up the twenty-five cents green fee. I remember John Meyers, Jim Fitzgerald, Doc Boone, and Howard Ewalt playing foursomes.

Jim, when teeing off, would step up to the ball, turn to his friends, and say, "Fellers, I'm gonna hit this 'un a fer piece."

Usually he did get a nice drive right down the middle.

Then John Meyers would tee up his ball. John had a hook that was hard to believe. He learned to play the hook rather than correcting it. On the old number seven hole his ball would leave the tee, take off northwest, then gradually curve back until his ball was moving in a northeast direction, eventually landing in the fairway.

Sorry, Morris, I got off the subject. I'll get back to The Cash Dry Goods. What I remember most about that store was the polished hardwood ladder in the shoe department. I'm sure you remember it. There was a metal rail along the top of the shelving. The top of the ladder had runners that rolled on the rail. The bottom of the ladder had two rubber-tired wheels. A slight shove sent the ladder rolling the entire length of the shelving. In the mid-1920s my mother used to take me there for shoes. I liked to watch as Mr. Meyers or Charlie McKinney, a longtime employee, rolled the ladder. (Mr. McKinney was the father of longtime Springdale mayor Charles N. McKinney.) I thought the ladder would be fun to play on. However, this pleasure I would never experience.

I also recall the beautiful brass National Cash Register. It was one of the fancy models, built on an oak base containing eight or ten cash drawers. Each clerk had his own drawer. When the Cash Dry Goods closed out, Dallas Barrack bought the register. It was still in Barrack's Gallery the last time I was there.

Later, The Cash installed one of those central cashier arrangements. I'm sure you remember—the cashier was up on the mezzanine. Wire cables ran from the cashier to different departments in the store. When the clerks made a sale, they put the sales ticket and money in a canister that traveled up the wire to the office. It worked on a spring-loaded mechanism. By pulling downward on a rope, the energy was transferred to a spring; then with a burst of energy, it sent the little trolley scooting up the wire. Return was by gravity. Most larger stores used similar arrangements until about 1950. The last ones I remember in Northwest Arkansas were at Penney's and at Campbell-Bell.

Well, I guess we have covered The Cash Dry Goods.

MORRIS CLARKSON

When we moved to the east side, there were a number of grocery stores in the area. West of us was a grocery owned by A. L. Clem. It was in a building that was later occupied by Oglesby Drug. Jim Oglesby bought two or three buildings in there and remodeled them into his new drug store.

Scott Watts had a grocery across the street from us. Shorty Parsons worked for Scott Watts. Then Shorty left Scott and bought our grocery store. It was in the west half of our original building. That was when we built the east part of our building and moved the dry goods into it. This was in the late '30s.

Soon after Shorty Parsons bought our store, Scott Watts sold his store to Donaldson's. East of Donaldson's was the cafe; it has been there forever, under different names. East of the cafe (#132) was Masoner's Grocery (#133). The Masoner store was the first building west of V. Price's station and produce. It was an old wooden frame building with a gable roof and wooden floor. (This was later the East Side Recreation Parlor—Author.)

Down on the corner of Emma and Park, east of Layman's, was a little filling station. It was a Southland station, located in a small wooden frame building owned by Collie Holt. He had a grocery store in conjunction with the station. Collie built a new home about three blocks north of his station, on the corner of Huntsville and Berry. The church now owns that property, and the Holt house has been moved or torn down. It is now part of the church parking lot.

By the way, we even had an oil well in Springdale. I don't suppose you could call it that, because they never hit oil. It was drilled on what is now the northeast corner of our airport. I can remember it was out behind the old Scott residence. At the time, there was quite a lot of excitement about it. The Famous Hardware had a jar of rock samples displayed in its front window.

(I never realized we came that close to being an oil town—Author.)

———

That little corner building (#110), the pie-shaped one directly across from the Jeff Brown building, was owned by Mr. Dampf. Do you remember him?

Yes, I remember Mr. Dampf. He was blind and ran a produce business on the east side there somewhere. My granddad (Charlie Vaughan) and Mr. Dampf were partners in the produce business for a time. When Charlie bought into the produce, he moved to Springdale and bought a stucco house on Maple. After Charlie sold the house, the stucco was covered with a brick veneer. You probably remember the house as the John Late property. Recently, the hospital acquired the property for a parking lot. The house was moved somewhere out near Beaver Lake.

MORRIS CLARKSON

I remember that Mr. Dampf had his desk in the front window of the produce. Any time I passed, it seemed he was always busy writing letters. He was a whiz on the typewriter.

> *Next door to the Dampf produce was Jeff Brown's Hatchery (#111). Later, the*
> *hatchery moved across the street (#114), and the building became a poultry lab.*
> *John Tyson's hatchery was east of the Jeff Brown building (#114).*

Shortly after the Lindbergh flight, sometime during the early years of the Great Depression, Brown's bought a bunch of balsa wood model airplanes to give away.

Every time I came to Springdale, I would ask Dad to stop and let me go in Jeff Brown's business office. Somewhat timid and embarrassed, I would go in and ask for a "glider." It seemed I always talked to Jim Murphy. I remember Jim's looking at me and saying, "I might find one around here somewhere." He would then stoop down behind the counter; a few seconds later he would stand up and hand me another one of the airplanes. I was never turned down.

MORRIS CLARKSON

> *You know the Barrack building (#61) was used as a auction building before*
> *Barrack moved in there with used furniture. This was in the Depression years,*
> *back in the early to mid-thirties. It was not a retail business; they opened up one*
> *night a week for an auction.*
>
> *I was always in town; my parents were at work in the store. Kid-like, I spent*
> *a lot of time looking around town, sticking my nose in this building, then*
> *another. One of my favorite loafing places was The Bear Cat Station.*
>
> *One day after leaving The Bear Cat, I walked down to the auction house to*
> *see what was going on there. I went in—and they had an old, square grand*
> *piano in there. I looked it over carefully, then ran over to the store. My dad was*
> *busy working in the back room.*
>
> *"They have a old grand piano down at the auction house, Dad. I would sure*
> *like to have it."*
>
> *"That's fine, Son, but what would you do with it?" he asked.*
>
> *"I thought I would bring it over here to the store," I answered.*
>
> *He didn't think too much of that idea but agreed to walk back to the auction*
> *house with me. We went in; there was no one there but the owner. Dad asked*
> *him what he intended to do with the piano.*
>
> *"It'll sell at auction this weekend, along with all the other stuff in here," he*
> *replied.*
>
> *Dad thought a moment, then said, "Would you consider selling it for cash*
> *right now? I don't think I can come to the sale."*
>
> *The man hesitated. "Tell you what—give me $12.50 for it, and it's yours,"*
> *he said.*
>
> *Dad paid him on the spot. It was a Steinway Grand. I still have it. It's a fine*
> *piano.*

Drug stores had some rough times years ago. Owning a drug store is no guarantee of success today, but our pioneer druggists made a profit the old-fashioned way: hard work and long hours.

Soda fountains, a favorite subject of nostalgic old-timers like myself, served a very real purpose in our community. They supported drug stores.

MARY LAWRENCE (April 1994)

Steve and I bought the old Applegate Drug Store in January 1948. We bought the store from Maggie (Applegate).

We depended on sales of merchandise and the soda fountain to support the store. Prescription sales were almost nothing.

Upstairs, across Emma Avenue, Dr. John Dorman was practicing with Dr. Friedman Sisco in the Sisco Clinic. Dr. A. J. Harrison was doing limited practice; because of his advanced age and bad health, he limited his practice to a few old friends.

Dr. Harrison seldom wrote a prescription, and the Sisco Clinic dispensed drugs from its own pharmacy.

Mary is, of course, speaking of the doctors on Emma Avenue.

Dr. Stanley Applegate moved to Springdale soon after the war and opened his medical practice in the Migratory Labor Camp Clinic in southeast Springdale. Perhaps this is a good time to mention the labor camp.

Northwest Arkansas, up until the 1960s, was primarily agricultural. The move toward an industrial economy is a recent trend.

During the spring, summer, and early fall we had a great need of temporary farm laborers. Living conditions and health care of these migratory workers was of concern to both our city government and the federal government.

In the mid-1940s a camp, similar to those used by the Armed Forces, was built on city property near the northwest corner of the airport, where Park Street intersects Caudle Street.

The camp consisted of neat rows of winterized tents. Each shelter had a wooden floor, wooden walls up about four feet, then screen wire. Canvas covered the top of the huts. Wooden shutters covered the screening. When lifted, they also served as a nice awning. It was bare minimum housing, but far better than sleeping in a barn or on the ground with no shelter at all.

In the center of the compound was a clinic, offices, recreation hall, church, and other facilities to help ease the hardships of underpaid workers.

In later years, housing facilities were upgraded to some extent; however, the living conditions remained basic.

Those who worked within the camp were driven more by compassion and dedication than they were by profit. Dr. Stanley Applegate spent several years at the camp.

DR. STANLEY APPLEGATE (July 26, 1994)

I offered walk-in, walk-out childbirth at the clinic in the labor camp. During my years there, I delivered over one hundred babies. The mothers walked in and, after the baby was born, walked out carrying a newborn baby.

In 1949, I entered into a partnership with Dr. Ralph Powers and Dr. John Dorman. Our offices were located in the building across from the city hall (#63) on Spring Street.

Jim Cheyne, the architect, was commissioned to design a new clinic for us. Our new facilities were completed in 1954.

In 1954, Dr. John Dorman, Dr. Ralph Power, and Dr. Stanley Applegate moved into the Springdale Clinic at the corner of Blair and Meadow.

It is highly unlikely that younger readers of this book will ever experience the compassion and dedication exhibited by doctors like Sisco, Powers, Dorman, Applegate, and Harrison. Perhaps one short story will illustrate my point.

When my oldest child, Mike, was fourteen months old, he fell on our front porch, hitting his head on a concrete step. It put a nice-size dent in his forehead.

Some weeks later our worries began. Our son would awaken from a sound sleep, often running through the house, perhaps falling, while uttering peculiar sounds. We found it difficult to awaken him, and, though he seemed to be talking, his sounds seldom made sense.

Dr. Applegate, our family doctor, was out of town. I explained my son's actions to Dr. John Dorman.

Dr. Dorman asked if Mike had ever had a blow to the head. I told him about the fall on our front porch and showed him the little crease in his forehead.

Dr. Dorman explained that it could be epileptic seizures that my son was having. He said they were sometimes caused by a blow to the head.

The nocturnal ordeals continued. Mary and I were deeply concerned. Often we did not go to bed. We preferred sitting up, waiting for the almost nightly episode to begin.

Once again we explained our problem to Dr. Dorman.

"There is only one way I can diagnose his case," he said. "I must examine him while he is actually having one of his—whatever it is that he is having. I will be at your house at 9:00 tonight. You and I will sit up all night. If I can see one of these spells, I am sure I can help."

Promptly at 9:00 P.M., Dr. Dorman arrived at our house. "Put on the coffee pot," he said. "It's going to be a long night."

About 2:30 A.M. we heard Mike scramble out of bed. He came running through the house, making the weird sounds.

I remember that Dr. Dorman asked for an ice cube. He placed it somewhere on the back of Mike's head or neck. He was able to examine him thoroughly before Mike became coherent.

"You have a sleep walker," said Dr. Dorman. "Nothing serious at all. He will grow out of it in a few years in all probability. Meanwhile, if you would like, I can give him some medicine that will produce a sounder sleep. You can use it for a short time and see if it helps. I think it will."

It was 4:00 A.M. when Dr. Dorman left for home. Needless to say, Mary and I were greatly relieved.

Oh, the doctor's fee for the all night visit? Just his fee for a regular house call—less than ten dollars, if I remember correctly.

Then there was the time during the Asian flu epidemic when Mary and I and all our children were so sick we could not get out of the house. Dr. Applegate came by every two days and had a nurse from the clinic come by daily with shots and medicine—but that is a rather long story.

Most residents of our city can tell you stories of how one or another of our doctors often went far beyond what was expected of him. Springdale owes so much to them.

I remember the old Sisco Clinic. It was over the Arkansas Western Gas Company (#49). Two examining rooms faced Emma. The waiting room occupied the mid-part of the building, and behind the waiting room was an x-ray room, a small laboratory, and three or four rooms for what we now call outpatient surgery. In fact, it was a miniature hospital, though I don't know that patients were kept overnight.

The wall between the two examining rooms was covered, floor to ceiling, with shelves for medicine. I well remember the dozens of brown bottles stored there; many of them were gallon size or larger. When Dr. C. P. Sisco finished examining a patient, he would reach for a bottle and pour out some medicine—sometimes pills or maybe a liquid. "Here, take this," he would say. "Pay Lucy two dollars on your way out."

MARY LAWRENCE (APRIL 20, 1994)

Yes, the only prescriptions they (Sisco, Dorman, and Harrison) wrote were for narcotics. This was not enough to keep a drug store in business. Percy Braun, a pharmacist, was employed by Applegate's when we bought the store. I understand he had been with them a long, long time.

We had no choice but to let him go. It was a sad choice for us, but there was simply not enough prescription business to warrant two registered pharmacists. There was no way we could afford to pay someone to fill prescriptions if there were no prescriptions to fill. It was a survival decision.

There were other problems: that drug store was one of the oldest stores in town and everything in it was worn out. The fountain was all but beyond repair. We spent a lot of money just keeping things going.

We sold to Rudy Moore in April of 1953. The doctor had told Steve to slow down. As you know, there is no way to run a retail store and slow down at the same time.

Delana Smith had a beauty shop on the mezzanine of Applegate's at one time. When we bought the store she was no longer there. I am not sure when she left. The only thing that was in our store, other than the drug store, was the liquor store. Gene Shaw bought the liquor stock. He asked us if he could keep it in our store until he found a location, preferably in the same block.

Gene moved up the street, west of Lichlyter's. He called his place The Smoke

Shop. (If I remember correctly, Gene told me he picked that name because some people felt uncomfortable being in business in the same block with a liquor store. Oddly enough, they were perfectly at ease with a tobacco store which sold liquor—Author.)

MARY LAWRENCE

We had been in business two or three years when the big flood hit downtown Springdale. I remember the soda fountain at Penrod's floating out the front window, and of course it ruined the organ at the Apollo. We escaped with no damage. Our store was an inch or so above the water.

You know, Dallas Barrack had a store full of valuable furniture and antiques. He was bringing in load after load from Chicago and Detroit. He had customers coming from all the surrounding states to do business with him. I am sure his damage was considerable. I have a couple of antique end tables that I was fortunate enough to buy from him.

We had some very rough years. It is only natural that people trade with long established merchants. Near us on the west was Roy Joyce (Joyce's Drug Store). Like his slogan said, he had "Been Here Always."

Down the block, to the east of us, was Coger's Drug. Mr. and Mrs. Coger put that store in just after the turn of the century, I believe. Cliff Samuel worked for him. Cliff had a lot of friends.

Across the railroad tracks, Jim Oglesby had been there since 1935 or so. He had one of the nicest drug stores in the area.

Morris Clarkson mentioned the Dampf produce building (#110) early in this chapter. From the mid-1930s until 1943, it was the home of Oglesby's Drug.

Mary Lawrence has told us of the problems a druggist faced in Springdale in the late 1940s. You can well imagine how much more difficult it was in the mid-1930s when Jim Oglesby opened a drug store in the little building, only feet from a railroad siding.

The railroad served as a dividing line for Springdale from the time the first train passed through our city. West of the railroad was known as "downtown Springdale." East of the tracks was known simply as "the East Side." This was not a cultural dividing line as some seem to think. Commerce east of the tracks was largely industrial, specifically: trucking, poultry and related activity, fresh produce, and agricultural supplies. The East Side had a limited number of retail business establishments. West of the tracks, business was almost 100% retail, banking, and professional services.

In 1935–36, when Jim Oglesby moved to Springdale, we had three practicing doctors of medicine: Dr. C. P. Sisco (Friedman was in medical school), Dr. R. T. Henry, and Dr. A. J. Harrison. We had an equal number of drug stores: Applegate's, Joyce's, and Coger's.

As Mary pointed out, Dr. Sisco dispensed almost all his own drugs. Dr. Henry was within feet of Joyce's and Applegate's. Dr. Harrison had a limited practice and was close to Coger's.

A short time after opening his drug store, Jim Oglesby was known to most everyone in town. He looked for, and found, a soft spot in the thick skin of Springdale business. Jim offered the best, and the cheapest, milk shakes and ice cream sodas in the city. Remember—the Depression, while less devastating, was still a constant companion of almost every citizen. Downtown workers earned from ten to twelve dollars a week. A salary of fifteen dollars weekly was considered high pay. If workers could save twenty cents on their noonday meal, that added up to almost five dollars a month. It was like getting a 10% raise.

I don't suppose that Mr. Oglesby made very much profit on a fifteen cent milk shake, but he got a lot of people through his store. If enough of them came in every day for a milk shake, it was only natural some would bring their prescriptions to him to be filled.

By 1943, east of his original store near the tracks, Jim Oglesby built one of the finest drug stores in Northwest Arkansas (#119–120).

CHAPTER 7

The Floods of Change

Events in the past may be roughly divided into those which prob-
ably never happened and those which do not matter. That is
what makes the trade of historian so attractive.

W. R. INGE (1860–1954)
DEAN OF ST. PAUL'S, LONDON

Mill Street is aptly named; it was one of the main routes leading to the Petross Grist Mill. South of Huntsville street, east of the Searcy home, Mill Street crossed the gravel-covered creek bed at an oblique angle. A century ago, horse drawn vehicles going to and from the mill kept the ground well-packed.

In my lifetime, the stream has been referred to by many names: Spring Creek, the Town Branch, "that d___ drainage ditch," and a few names I would hesitate to commit to paper.

The small gently-curving brook was delightful in the spring when wild flowers covered its banks, and large oaks arching gracefully over the rippling stream shaded its crystal clear water. Picnickers found its attractions irresistible.

During our dry, hot summer months, the small creek dwindled to a mere trickle. In the winter, when its grassy, sloping banks were snow-covered, it had an enchanting beauty, becoming, in fact, the "winter wonderland" extolled by countless writers of flowery prose.

And in the fall, when our trees achieved their peak colors of red, gold, and yellow, the stream assumed all the beauty of an old master's painting. But when it rained— and rained hard (I mean one of those toad-strangling gully washers)—watch out! The small stream could very quickly become a raging torrent of muddy water rushing northward, carrying with it tons of accumulated debris tossed in the creek by some of our less environmentally conscious residents.

This small gentle stream, in my opinion, is the catalyst that changed downtown Springdale forever. Whether the change was for better or worse will be determined by future historians. For the present, let's just say that the change was inevitable. Some stories persist that Divine Intervention was a factor. Whether or not such stories are true is a matter of conjecture. If there is a master plan to our universe, as most of us believe, I see no logical reason why the plan should not include downtown Springdale.

Business firms migrated to Emma Avenue well before the turn of the century, making it our primary, indeed our only, retail thoroughfare. The reasons why business firms chose this particular part of our city are many and complex. The settlement was not laid out that way originally.

Some of our younger citizens might explain it this way: "Like, man, you know, we all gotta be somewhere, you know what I'm sayin'?"

For the purpose of this story, let it suffice to say that it happened. Gradually business buildings appeared along the dirt street. Spring Creek bisected Emma Avenue, presenting a rather annoying problem near the center of our budding metropolis. Let's be candid—at times the center of town became a giant mudhole.

It became evident that a bridge across the creek was badly needed. A by-product of such an improvement was the additional building spaces a bridge would provide in the downtown area. What better place to locate a store than over the little creek? When the bridge was completed, most shoppers would not realize the stream existed.

Then, as now, plans for the abatement of immediate problems seldom included the future. A passageway under our shopping district, thought adequate at the time, remained constant in size, while the water flow increased yearly. As new homes were built and more streets paved, the runoff increased tremendously. Springdale's growth was on a collision course with nature or, if you prefer, with the Almighty.

A man of the cloth, residing south of Emma Avenue, was the pastor of a small church near Springdale. He took great pride in his calling, his home, his family, and the vegetable garden behind his modest home. The rows in his garden were straight, his plants evenly spaced, and not a weed could be found anywhere. There was one thing that annoyed him: at the back of his garden, tilted at a precarious angle, stood a long unused outhouse, an unsightly tribute to years gone by. This unpainted structure presented a potential hazard; it could, with the aid of a strong south wind, fall into his tomato patch.

This dilapidated privy was a constant reminder of his lean years of the 1930s. Now, entering the 1950s, he had indoor plumbing. The Lord had seen fit to deliver His people from those unforgotten, extremely unpleasant trips to those picturesque little houses that once graced the back yard of every home.

With the advent of modern plumbing, we gained comfort and convenience, but lost a valuable part of childhood training, especially our reflexes. Absolutely nothing in this world will increase your sense of alertness and speed of reaction more, than hearing the rattle of a snake less than two feet below your bare posterior. Some may argue that the sting of a red wasp is equally effective. I digress . . .

Our good citizen, overflowing with civic pride, decided to improve the appearance of his property. The old outhouse was pushed over, flooding his mind with memories of Halloweens past—when he was a carefree country boy. The remains of the structure were deposited in a heap near the Frisco tracks. There they remained until the fateful night of May 29, 1950.

Sam Bryant finished his last haircut of the day, tossed some towels and aprons in the laundry box, and put away the tools of his trade. "Jesse, it looks like we may get some rain tonight; the radio says it might even storm. I'm going on home before it starts." Sam looked at his watch. It was just past 6:30 P.M.

Jesse Camden, a lifelong resident of Springdale, was the general clean-up man for the Palace Barber Shop. In exchange for his janitorial duties, he received a small salary and was allowed to sleep in the back room. His meager possessions consisted of a small cot, an old two-burner gas stove, and a coffee pot.

Jesse finished cleaning up the shop about 7:30 P.M. Glancing toward the street, he noticed people standing in front of Penrod's, watching the storm front move in from the west. He stepped outside. The dark clouds looked like any other spring rain; in his opinion it was nothing to worry about.

As he watched, lightning flashes became more frequent and appeared much closer. Booming thunder became louder; rumbling in from the west, it rolled down Emma and disappeared in the general direction of the sale barn. Large drops of rain began falling before dark, each drop splattering as it hit the warm sidewalk. Jesse went back inside, locked the door, and retired to his little room in the back. He tried listening to the radio for a few minutes, but the static was so bad he decided to go to bed. Before 9:00 the drumming of heavy rain on the tar-paper roof lulled him into a sound sleep.

On West Emma Avenue, in front of the new Apollo Theater, patrons sat in their cars watching the approaching storm while waiting for the ticket window to open. Those arriving before show time could enjoy up to thirty minutes of music played on the mighty pipe organ. Mr. Sonneman's daughter-in-law, Gladys, was the organist, and she was one of the best around.

In the well-appointed lobby, a marble statue of the Greek God Apollo, unmindful of his lack of attire, welcomed the public to our finest movie house. In mythology, Apollo was the god of Music, Poetry, and Prophecy; he also represented Youth and Beauty. The story of Apollo's journey from a smoke-filled northern city to the lobby of a small theater in Arkansas is intriguing.

Dallas Barrack owned a number of buildings on Mill Street, just north of Emma (#26–61). In the mid-1940s, Dallas opened a retail furniture store. Immediately after the war new merchandise was in short supply, but used furniture was readily available. Though he sold both new and used, very soon Barrack's became known as the place to find good used furniture at very attractive prices.

Barrack's employed the services of a professional "picker" in the Chicago area. A picker is someone, employed by an individual or business, to search for—and buy—a certain type of merchandise. The picker normally has a warehouse where such items are stored until picked up by the buyer. Barrack's moved a tremendous quantity of merchandise from the Chicago area back to Springdale. Dallas found it necessary to purchase a large moving van and to employ a full-time driver.

Much of the merchandise was from large estates and private collections. In a short time the quality of goods sold by Barrack's changed. Common used furniture was replaced by fine antiques and the better works of art. Barrack's Furniture evolved into Barrack's Gallery. Dallas Barrack is extremely knowledgeable in his field. He made it possible for people of modest income to enjoy treasures that once were prized possessions of only the very wealthy.

In 1947, only days after Mary and I were married, we bought a new red and white breakfast set from Barrack's. It was all metal, made by Arvin Industries, and cost us $49.95.

Two weeks later we had our first argument. I bought a beautiful solid oak, five section, office-type bookcase from Barrack Furniture for $20. When I carried it into our small apartment, Mary started crying.

"How are we ever going to get ahead if you are going to waste our money on junk?" she asked.

It was a good question. It remains unanswered forty-six years later. By the way, we still have the bookcase. Its value today is about $800.

Another example: Mrs. Knox of the Knox Gelatin financial empire loved fine antiques. She toured the world looking for treasures for her home. When her mansion was filled and could accommodate no more antiques, she locked it up and bought another mansion. At the time of her death she had six large mansions, filled to overflowing with art and antiques. Everything was sold. The auction lasted several months.

I happened to be visiting with Dallas in his store when his first van of antiques from the Knox estate arrived. I watched as they started unloading. I especially liked one large piece still inside the van. Quickly I ran up to the First National Bank.

"Mary, you have got to come down to Barrack's and see what Dallas has on his truck," I said. "It's one of the prettiest pieces of furniture you will ever see."

Mary was becoming accustomed to my fits of enthusiasm for antiques. I could tell she did not share my excitement. However, she consented to come and take a look. Well, she loved the piece. We decided to buy it, if we could possibly afford it.

It was a large china cabinet, made of solid mahogany and lined with bird's-eye maple. The doors were beveled glass, and all hardware was solid brass. The piece looked like new and weighed several hundred pounds.

"How much for that monstrosity inside your truck?" I asked.

Dallas blinked his eyes at me a couple of times and answered, "Give me sixty-five dollars, and I'll leave it on board. When we've finished unloading, I'll deliver it direct to your house."

We still call it the monstrosity, and today it is worth more than I paid for it . . . much more.

Well, let's get back to Bill Sonneman and his theater. Mr. Sonneman owned most of the theaters in this area. When he began construction of his third Springdale theater (I believe the year was 1948), he wanted it to be the flagship of his movie theater fleet. His new motion picture house would be second to none.

A real pipe organ, one of the best ever to be heard in our fair city, had been completely refurbished and installed in the theater. Not one of those electronic gadgets, but a honest-to-God, genuine, no-holds-barred pipe organ. It was equipped with everything from real bass drums to tambourines. Few theaters outside the larger cities boasted any better. The magnificent console was placed down front, dead center. Mr. Sonneman wanted the organist to be seen as well as heard.

Max Cox was Mr. Sonneman's theater manager in Springdale. Max had years of construction experience before going to work for Mr. Sonneman. It was only logical that he would be involved in building the theater.

Construction was almost completed, yet the new theater was without a name. One day Max mentioned to his boss that Dallas Barrack had a beautiful statue of Apollo in his store. Bill rushed down to Barrack's and struck a deal for its purchase. In one day, he acquired an artistic center of attraction for the lobby, plus a name befitting his latest palace of imagination. Springdale's citizens eagerly awaited the opening of the Apollo. I feel fortunate to have been in attendance opening night.

The theater, still standing, was built over a drainage ditch just east of the Callison-Sisco Funeral Home.

It's now 11:00 P.M. The rainfall continues, sometimes quite heavy. Drainage ditches are beginning to reach flood stage. Runoff from the south is steadily increasing. Behind the neat home of our good preacher, his garden is now under water. The surging water tugs at a board from his old outhouse. Suddenly it breaks free, tumbling and turning in the roiling waters as it gains momentum. Another board succumbs to the raging current. Before the first board passes behind the old Dr. Christian house, the entire outhouse is afloat, headed for the Meadow Street bridge.

Floating boards from the privy are joined by other debris. Unfortunately, in its mad rush downstream, the oversize pile of trash becomes lodged under the bridge. Water starts rising; more trash is picked up and carried to the narrow passage. Rapidly-rising water reaches the Pioneer Lumber Company. Dimension lumber floats from the lumber yard out onto Emma Avenue. Larger pieces of floating lumber break through plate-glass windows of several buildings.

Jesse, asleep on his cot in the Palace Barber Shop, hears glass shattering. Is someone breaking in? As his mind clears, he becomes aware of a lot of loud yelling and talking. Apparently something is happening out on Emma. He sits up in bed and swings his feet to the floor. He finds he is standing in water. Only then does Jesse realize that water is floating his bed. His shoes are nowhere to be found. Jesse pulls on his soaked trousers and hurries outside—barefoot. Looking around at all the broken glass, he realizes that he must get some shoes on. He wades back in the barber shop; his shoes are floating in the flood waters near his bed.

Hurrying back outside, he is surprised to see chairs and a showcase float through Penrod's front window. Inside the cafe a large deep freeze, recently installed, is floating toward the front window. Devastation and confusion are widespread. Jesse wants to help. He returns to the Palace, and as an item floats within reach, he grabs it and places it on the back bar.

TOM BAIN (MARCH 1994)

About 2:00 A.M. I received a telephone call from Shelby Ford. "Tom," he said, "they called just now and told me the bank is washing away. Would you get down there real fast and see what's going on?"

Well, I hadn't been with the bank very long. It sounded like Shelby, but the thought crossed my mind that it might be someone trying to lure me to the bank for a holdup.

The more I thought about it, the more positive I was that it was Shelby on the phone. I got up, dressed, and started to town. We lived out on Mill then; it was not very far to drive.

I got as far as the Long-Bell Lumber Company. When I got there, lumber was floating out in the street. I realized I had driven as far as I could. I parked my car and started wading in knee-deep water.

When I got to the bank, water was flowing through the building—coming in through the front and flowing out the back.

I stepped back out on the street and watched chairs and tables float out of Penrod's cafe through the broken front windows. I suppose water had pushed the plate glass windows out.

We had a water pump in the basement of the bank. It never stopped running, even though it was under six feet of water.

Max Cox walked upstairs to the Apollo projection room. He glanced at the movie reels, estimating how much longer the feature would run. He was relieved to see it was almost over. He decided to cancel the second feature. As usual, when cancellation of the second feature was necessary, he would have the projectionist run the newsreel, comedy, and previews of coming attractions again for the convenience of those who arrived late.

His back was hurting. He wanted to get home, take a couple of aspirin, and go to bed. Max had suffered chronic back problems ever since he was hurt on a construction job some fifteen years before.

Max closed the box office and hung out a sign announcing the cancellation of the second feature.

The first trickle of water appeared near the front of the theater, shortly before the house lights came on. The slowly growing puddle of water was under the stage, where the floor was lowest.

Max said goodnight to the projectionist, checked all exits, pulled the big switch, and locked the front door behind him. Ten minutes later he was in his comfortable home at 621 West Allen (immediately north of the Springdale Memorial Hospital Heliport).

Near 11:30 P.M. (a calculated estimate), debris lodges in the drainage ditch under the Apollo. Sometime after midnight the organ console is lifted from the floor by rising water. Electrical wires snap, air hoses break, and the organ console floats free.

Near morning, when the falling waters deposit the once beautiful console on the soggy carpet near the stage, it is little more than junk. Cost of restoration is prohibitive. Springdale citizens will never again hear the sound of a pipe organ in their movie house. The motion picture business is changing. An era, once thought of as eternal, just ended. The world will never see its like again. And such a pity . . .

From *The Springdale News,* May 30, 1950

FLASH FLOOD INUNDATES DOWNTOWN STORES
CLOUDBURST SENDS FOUR-FOOT WALL OF WATER ON EMMA

Roaring torrents of water swept into downtown district last night and early this morning causing tens of thousands of dollars of water damage.

Water extended from west of the railroad tracks to Holcomb Street. Merchants near the Spring Creek ditch were especially hard-hit. They included: Clark-Deaver Hardware, Hallock Grocery, OTASCO, Penrod's, Ellis Ice Cream Parlor, S. R. Wilson Mercantile, Economy Shoe Store, Coger's Drug, Publix Market, Camp's, Coleman Shoe Store, First National Bank, First State Bank, Lively Jewelry, Palace Barber Shop, the Concord Theater, the Apollo Theater, and Springdale Taxi Service. Stout Condra Auto Parts and Burt's Furniture suffered basement damage. Five feet of water filled the Bargain Center. It was declared a total loss. The OTASCO warehouse and Clark-Deaver warehouse in the same area also suffered extensive damage.

Families living behind the First Baptist Church, including the Ray Tabor and the Jim King families, were rescued by boat. The boat was manned by Bobby Eidson and Jim Webb. Fire Chief Ralph Brooks and Bobby Brooks assisted occupants of flooded homes to safety.

Timbers were found lodged against the Meadow Street bridge. The rain began at 8:00 P.M. last night and continued until 1:30 A.M. this morning.

Autry Wilson was one of the first merchants to take advantage of the flood. I suspect he acted more by necessity than by planning. As employees started carrying soggy merchandise upstairs from the basement, they had trouble finding any place to put it. Someone thought of putting tables in front of the store on the sidewalk. A quickly-lettered FLOOD SALE sign appeared on Wilson's windows.

By good daylight the following morning, Emma Avenue was filled with anxious merchants and curious residents, eager for a first-hand look at the widespread damage. They were attracted to the tables in front of Wilson's like flies to a picnic. Several clerks kept busy selling water-soaked clothing at prices only a little below full retail price. Everyone caught the bargain hunter fever. I bought a pair of rubber boots for which I had absolutely no use. The only BS I had to wade through was around the coffee drinkers' tables in Penrod's. To the best of my memory, I saved fifty cents on the purchase and never wore the boots once—but I had bought a bargain.

Wilson's sold out of merchandise they had long ago written off as unsalable. It seemed as though an invisible force overcame us, wiping out our compassion and judgement and creating within us a panic to buy wet clothing—and all simply because so many people, myself included, wanted to profit by a friend's loss.

The week following the flood, a story making the rounds among coffee drinkers at Penrod's concerned a well-known Emma merchant whose store was on slightly higher ground. He arrived downtown before daylight that unfortunate morning. He was pleased to find his store had escaped with practically no damage. For this he was thankful, but as he stood in front of Penrod's watching Autry Wilson selling twenty-year-old long drawers and overalls, he realized he was missing a golden opportunity.

He watched with a twinge of envy, as the mad scramble around Wilson's outdoor tables continued. Happy buyers left the rickety wooden tables carrying load after load of soggy clothing. He pondered his dilemma—then sprang into action.

Quickly he returned to his store. "Put two of these old tables out front on the sidewalk and put this one in the alley," he said. "Be quick about it! We are going to have a sale!"

Grabbing his sign-making kit, he wrote the words FLOOD SALE on a eight-foot length of white wrapping paper.

Turning to his help, he said, "Carry all these overalls out back. Put them on the table, and don't ask questions. Wait for my word before putting that sign up."

Our enterprising merchant then hooked up his window-washing hose in the alley and proceeded to wet down his first table of "flood-damaged clothing."

Very soon he had both tables out front full of dripping goods. Then the sign went up, and the crowds arrived. One person kept busy wetting down clothing, as another carried the dripping loads through the store to the tables on the sidewalk. Sure, it was messy—but there's supposed to be water on the floor after a flood.

Actually, when the flood damage was cleaned up, it was found that most firms had less dollar loss than first estimated. However, a hue and cry went up to do something about our terrible problems. Then, as now, money was a factor. The cost of properly engineering a drainage system through our downtown area seemed prohibitive. The city did not have that kind of reserve. The problem was put on the back burner, more or less. Most members of our city council hoped the problem would, like General MacArthur, just fade away.

In the mid-1950s, when word arrived that Springdale could possibly qualify for urban renewal money, most of our movers and shakers were overjoyed. After all, if the government pays for it, it doesn't cost anyone anything. Oddly enough, the same form of reasoning continues today.

I am sure no one will be surprised when I say that some who worked hardest for urban renewal, as well as some who violently opposed the plan, were influenced by selfish motives. Is it not the same with every governmental project?

Few could deny that many of our downtown business buildings needed rebuilding. Our drainage system was a carry over from the turn of the century. Downtown parking was a problem. Yes, we had problems aplenty . . .

TOM BAIN (MARCH 1994)

When I was offered a position with the First State Bank back in '47, I was not sure I wanted to move to Springdale. My wife and I came up here on several weekends to look over the town.

The things I remember most were the old sheet-iron awnings on front of downtown buildings. Some were spotted with rust; some had corners bent where trucks had hit them; and it seemed every post supporting the awnings was bent where some car had jumped the curb.

Then there were all the trucks with strawberries and grapes lined up for blocks along Emma. Mixed in with the produce trucks, eighteen-wheelers loaded with chickens worked their way through the stalled traffic. And, of course, every fourth truck seemed to be orange and black, Jones Truck Lines colors. There was far too much traffic for one narrow street.

Other factors, mostly a result of increasing population, were of prime consideration. A migration of retail business firms from downtown Springdale to the suburbs started soon after the war. Only by leaving the downtown area could merchants acquire much larger buildings with adequate parking, a top priority if they were to survive the coming years. The days of the 20-foot wide store buildings were coming to an end. By the mid-1950s, the trend initiated by a few merchants became a general exodus.

However, vacated spaces were badly needed for expansion of Springdale's financial and legal establishments. For example, both the First State and First National banks were growing at warp speed. In the late 1940s each bank had less than twelve employees. Today, over 300 people are employed by our two oldest banks. Springdale, a small agricultural community, was fulfilling the wildest dreams of our chamber of commerce and was on its way to becoming a city of manufacturing and commerce.

Urban renewal happened; our downtown area is no longer in danger of flooding.

Yet, there are those among us who miss the small shops and Saturday night crowds. Emma Avenue, like the rest of the world, has changed. I hope this book will help preserve Emma's colorful past—what a grand old street she was!

> *Striving to better, oft we mar what's well.*
>
> ALBANY, KING LEAR

Gunsmoke in the Parlor

A short history of radio
in Northwest Arkansas

*You have debased (my) child . . . You have made him a
laughing stock of Intelligence . . . a stench in the nostrils of the
Gods of the Ionosphere.*

DR. LEE DE FOREST (1873–1961)

So what, precisely, was this new business I had chosen to enter? Where did it come from? Where could I expect it to go in my lifetime? What were the origins of radio? Just how far into the future was the long-awaited invention of television?

It is said, "What man can imagine, man can accomplish." Would this old axiom apply to the emerging science of electronics? If so, the next twenty-five years would be difficult, trying to stay ahead of a facet of science suddenly thrown into warp speed by recent wartime developments.

It is human nature to associate one man's name with every new invention. Henry Ford, the automobile; Robert Fulton, the steamboat; F. B. Morse, the telegraph; Alexander Graham Bell, the telephone; Thomas A. Edison, the talking machine and electric lights; Daguerre, photography; and yes, Marconi invented radio. Oh, did he really? Well . . . more or less. Let's take a peep backward, then decide for ourselves.

Perhaps it all started in 600 B. C. when Thales experimented with rods of amber. He discovered that under certain conditions, like stroking the rod with a woolen cloth, certain peculiar properties of amber were exhibited. The Greek root of amber, some fifteen centuries later, gave us the word *electricity.* The word is first found in print in 1646 in Sir Richard Browne's *Pseudodoxio Epedemica.*

Pliny and Pliny the younger, without realizing what they were doing, used the properties of electric current in experiments carried out in the days of the Roman Empire.

Heinrich Hertz, in 1866, verified certain theories concerning electricity and magnetism, first advanced by the Scotsman James Clerk Maxwell. Hertz actually caused an electric spark to occur between two closely spaced electrodes connected to a induction coil and located some distance from a similar coil in which he induced a high tension electric current.

In 1885, Dr. Mahlon Loomis, a Washington, D. C., dentist, sent a kite aloft carrying a large square of very fine copper mesh. A slender copper wire trailed from the copper screen to earth. On another mountain eighteen miles away, a similar kite was launched. A galvanometer, connected in series between one kite and ground, indicated a needle movement when the wire from the kite on the distant mountain was connected and disconnected to a coil of wire buried in the ground. This experiment, utilizing static electricity in the air, could have been used to transmit messages in code had the dentist persevered.

Michael Faraday contributed many ideas to this new science. Alternating current, the electromagnetic theory of light, and the values of different dielectrics are just a few of his major discoveries.

All these experiments, plus many more, were accumulating in the reservoir of man's total knowledge, waiting for one man with imagination to apply them. With the invention of the telegraph, man began dreaming of sending telegraphic messages without the need of wires. Both Thomas Edison and Alexander Graham Bell were busy at work in their laboratories trying to unlock the secret of wireless telegraphy.

In Bologna, in 1874, an Irish mother and an Italian father became the proud parents of a son, whom they named Guglielmo. The young lad attended the Leghorn Technical Institute. Early on, he became a disciple of Professor Righi of the University of Bologna and developed an intense interest in inductive telegraphy.

When twenty years of age, he returned to his father's large estate outside the city of Bologna, where he could conduct experiments with electric wave phenomena. Here in the Italian countryside, using circuits and components available in most university laboratories, Marconi developed the concept from which radio would emerge.

It is true that Marconi invented nothing. He integrated several inventions of others into a workable system whereby he could transmit and receive messages over great distances—without wires. Hence came the name "wireless," as the new art would be known until the advent of broadcast radio.

Marconi took his equipment to Great Britain in 1896. On Salisbury Plain, he gave a demonstration during which he sent and received a wireless message over a distance of two miles. He filed for a British patent on June 2, 1896.

The reaction was immediate. Newspapers and magazines were quick to publish articles about this memorable scientific event. Many scientists, who had worked for years on the idea, tried to discredit Marconi. Edison was especially vehement. He was quick to point out that Marconi had invented nothing—that all he had done was apply the work of others. Though his charges were quite true, it was Marconi who utilized scientific knowledge available in 1896 and forged it into a workable system of communications. So, while not the inventor of wireless, Marconi can with certainty be called the Father of Radio, a term Dr. Lee De Forest wrongfully applied to himself.

By 1900, Marconi had increased the range of his equipment enough to span the English Channel. Just before noon on December 12, 1901, Marconi successfully sent the letter "S" across the Atlantic. Edison purchased a full page ad in the New York City papers, branding the whole event as a hoax.

With primitive equipment, unreliable and limited in range, Marconi founded the Wireless Telegraph and Signal Company in Great Britain and the American Marconi Company in the U. S. His business was marine communications—either ship to ship or ship to shore. The high conductivity of salt water resulted in a greater range than that of land-based stations. Still, communication was limited to a distance of some fifty miles and subject to static crashes, plus interference from other stations. Ideal conditions could, of course, result in much greater distances.

Detectors, the heart of any receiving set, were on the minds of all radio experimenters. Marconi used a Coherer Detector: a small glass tube, loosely packed with iron filings. In the period from 1903 to 1920, a hunk of unrefined lead, better known as "galena," was widely used. Most all boys growing up in those years constructed crystal sets using such a detector. At the time this was a standard Boy Scout project. Several articles on building crystal radios appeared in the twenties, wherein the authors suggested using a Quaker Oatmeal box as a coil form. Quaker Oats sales soared. Such radios became known as Quaker Oats sets.

In the late 1890s, Lee De Forest paid a visit to Professor Fessenden's laboratory in Canada. The trusting professor demonstrated a new detector, superior to the Coherer, to the American inventor. Returning to the states, Dr. De Forest promptly filed for a patent on what he called the Electrolytic Detector. He was widely acclaimed for "his" new invention and was quick to install it in all units he was manufacturing for the Navy.

Professor Fessenden was outraged and filed suit in the federal courts. The courts ruled in Fessenden's favor in 1906.

With the sinking of the "unsinkable" ship Titanic in 1912, wireless experienced a tremendous growth. International laws were rapidly passed requiring every vessel to have a wireless station on board with operators on duty twenty-four hours a day. A new bonanza opened up for wireless companies—the training of thousands of shipboard operators.

Marine installations, until well into the twenties, used spark transmitters and crystal receivers. Technology discovered some years before was still under development.

Indeed, as late as 1936 crystal radio receivers were required to be a part of every ship's equipment. While very limited in range, they were dependable, extremely simple, and required no external power supply. Incoming signals provided the only power used by crystal radios. Therefore, though the ship's power might fail, crystal radio receivers could still be used.

The Marconi Company made millions manufacturing shipboard wireless equipment. During the World War I era Mr. Marconi found it necessary to pay one full-time employee for the sole purpose of delivering flowers to his many mistresses around New York City. It is rumored the poor chap often had to work overtime.

In 1904, Ambrose Fleming inserted a square metal plate into a light bulb. He discovered that this "valve," as he called it, would act as a radio detector, the results being little better than a galena crystal.

Soon after the courts ruled that De Forest had patented Professor Fessenden's detector, the De Forest Company filed for bankruptcy, leaving De Forest with nothing but some equipment from his laboratory. Among this equipment was a Fleming Valve into which he had inserted another element—a zig-zag piece of wire. His stockholders allowed him to retain this gadget which they considered worthless. He called it the Audion. Though he had no idea how it worked, he discovered this "Audion" would actually amplify radio signals. Thus was born the vacuum tube, a invention destined to make radio a priority item in every home in America, though it would take almost twenty-five years to do so. The year was 1906.

While the Audion had the potential of amplifying radio signals, the detector circuits of 1905 were such that this potential was not utilized. Distant signals were weak and could be heard only through headphones. Horn-type speakers (loudspeakers) did not come into common use until 1922–25.

Radio amateurs are responsible for almost all of the developments that made radio a home entertainment medium. In 1912, a young amateur (ham operator) was experimenting in his bedroom (ham shack). It was early morning; the family was fast asleep. Suddenly, he let out a yell and ran to his sister's, then to his parent's bedroom. "I have done it! I have done it!" he yelled.

The family rushed to his room where a small vacuum tube radio was tuned to a wireless station. The signals were so loud the listeners had to hold the headphone some distance from their ears. Sets then had no volume controls; they had never before been needed. Edwin H. Armstrong had invented the regenerative radio circuit: a circuit that feeds the signal from the detector tube output, back into the tube's input—again and again, thousands of times—until the signal is amplified many times its original strength.

Dr. De Forest filed suit, claiming he invented the regenerative circuit. When called to the witness stand before other engineers and scientists, he became confused, unable to explain any part of its operation. Later, a judge in a higher court found in favor of De Forest. Every engineer, then and now, recognizes Armstrong as the true inventor of the regenerative circuit. Indeed, few in radio today associate De Forest with any invention other than the vacuum tube, and even there a sliver of doubt remains.

In his lifetime Dr. De Forest would "invent" and patent over two hundred ideas. Experts now believe most of his inventions were the work of his contemporaries. De Forest was an accomplished promoter; today he might be called a con artist. He organized over twenty companies from 1900 to 1927, all of which he would lead into bankruptcy. When he died in 1961, he had but $1,250 left in his bank account.

In 1918, Armstrong invented the superheterodyne circuit—a circuit employed in over 99% of all radios manufactured from 1930 until the present. Never content, he invented super-regeneration in 1922.

His greatest invention, FM (frequency modulation), came in the 1930s. Every television and the majority of radios in use today use FM sound. Sales and royalties from previous inventions made Armstrong the single largest stockholder in Radio Corporation of America. Unfortunately, the invention of FM would ultimately destroy him completely.

One point we must keep in mind—wireless was concerned with but one thing: transmitting a message from point A to point B. This concept changed forever in 1919 when another radio amateur, Dr. Frank Conrad, began "broadcasting" from his garage in Pittsburg, Pennsylvania. These messages, through his "phone" or modulated transmitter, were aimed at a general audience, not just a single listener. The broadcasts were intermittent in nature—usually a hour or so each day—and consisted of phonograph records, baseball scores, and news items. He was surprised to find that he had a number of listeners, mostly other radio amateurs and experimenters using simple crystal radios to hear the broadcasts.

A music store in downtown Pittsburg loaned Dr. Conrad records for his broadcasts. The store noticed they rapidly sold out of those records that Dr. Conrad played on his broadcasting set. There must be some connection! The store had a number of unsold World War I surplus radio sets in stock. The manager asked Dr. Conrad to please mention these sets on the air. Within a week they were completely sold out. Radio broadcasting and advertising were born.

In 1920, the Westinghouse Electric Company moved Dr. Conrad's broadcasting set to studios on the top floor of its building in Pittsburg and began broadcasting on a regular basis, using the call letters KDKA. By 1925 most cities in the United States had at least one radio station.

ROBERT "BOB" H. CLARK (OCTOBER 1993)

I had the first real radio in Springdale—not necessarily the first radio. Several boys around town were playing with crystal radios, with practically no success. I must have built a dozen. Occasionally you could hear one of the high-power spark transmitters sending code. That is all there was then.

I became interested in electricity when the town branch, as was its custom, flooded the basement of The Famous Hardware. Several dry cell batteries stored there had their cardboard covers ruined, rendering them unsalable. Dad asked me if I would like to have them. Of course, I was interested. He brought them home. I was curious to see whether they had any "life" left in them. I picked up a pair of pliers and shorted out the positive terminal to ground. Sparks flew all over my shop. I was so excited that I had no other thought in life but to find out everything I could about electricity. Dad was with me all the way.

In 1921, I was fifteen years old. We had been taking Radio News magazine for two or three years. We took two magazines: The American Boy and Radio

News. I sent off for an A. C. Gilbert Company catalog. (The Gilbert Company sold Erector sets, chemistry sets, radio and electrical supplies. The company was built on the scientific curiosity of young people—Author.)

Donovan Youree was my friend and fellow experimenter. He lived on the corner of Blair and Allen Streets. We had been building crystal sets with little or no success. Anyway, in the A. C. Gilbert catalog they had a one audion (tube) radio kit for sale. The tube had wires coming out of the top and bottom. I showed the ad to my dad and asked if I could have the audion receiver kit for Christmas.

Dad said, "You sure can, Son. I will see that you get it."

I built the set and kept fiddling around with it. Donovan had his crystal set. We learned the code and, using Model T coils as spark transmitters, communicated between our house on Thompson, across from the Lutheran Church, and Donovan's home on Allen. I strung my aerial, or antenna, from the top of the old water tower, behind our house on Johnson and Highway 71 to the barn that was just south of our house. The aerial was sixty feet long and consisted of four copper wires strung between six-foot cross arms located on each end. It was a handsome thing, glistening in the sun.

I had a telephone, but Donovan didn't. After we spent a hour or so each night transmitting messages in code, we would meet half way between our homes and compare notes to see how well we had done. Of course, we were operating without a license, and therefore illegally, but the government was rather lax about such things in 1921.

We loved to listen to the Rotary Spark Gap transmitter they had at the University of Arkansas amateur radio station. It would start with a low raspy note of about 60 cycles and gradually increase in frequency up to 600 cycles or so, as the rotary gap picked up speed. It made so much noise that they had to rig up a sound isolation room to house it.

I could pick up the Arlington time signals on the one-tube receiver. I got a lot of publicity on this. Jewelers and others would come to the house and set their watches by the signals.

I had my one-tube audion working good. I was sitting there one night, spinning the dial, when I heard a voice. You can imagine my surprise. Back then, there was nothing on the air but code transmitters. I was glued to that thing for at least a half hour. Finally I heard them say, "This is KDKA, Pittsburgh."

I was so flabbergasted—I had no idea I could reach that far. I ran downstairs and told my parents I was hearing voices on my radio. Dad said, "Let's go upstairs and take a look at that wondrous receiver."

I listened to see that KDKA was still coming through and handed Dad the head phone. He put it to his ear and listened and listened. We stood perfectly still; finally he lowered the little earphone. He looked at me with amazement and said, "Do you know what I just heard? I heard a Miss Birch from Argentina—a soprano—singing opera."

He sat down on a box and was quiet for some time. Then he said, "Son, is there some way we could have that louder so the family and friends could enjoy it?"

I was way ahead of him. "Dad," I said, "for $259 I can buy enough stuff to build a regenerative detector and two-step audio amplifier. That price would include one of the new Magnavox horn-type speakers."

I had the price figured to the penny. My prices were from the latest Tucker Duck and Rubber Company catalog. The Duck catalog was the prime reference and dream book for experimenters in the late teens and twenties.

Dad said, "Son, you take that catalog down to the store (The Famous Hardware) tomorrow and give it to Stant (Mr. Thompson). He's our bookkeeper.

Tell him to order everything you need and charge it to me."

Dad was anxious for the parts to arrive. When they came, I built the radio on a breadboard with the usual black Bakelite panel. When it was finished, I checked it out to be sure it was working, then called Dad upstairs to my attic workshop. He listened to it and just went crazy. After listening for awhile, he looked at me and said, "Son, that is amazing . . . but can't you make it look a little bit better?"

"Well, I guess so," I answered. He replied, "There is a excellent cabinetmaker downtown. Take it to him tomorrow and tell him to build a solid walnut cabinet for that radio. I want it to look as good as it sounds."

Well, I can't remember the cabinetmaker's name, but he built the prettiest walnut cabinet you can imagine. It was about thirty inches wide and had a hinged door across the top.

Every night our living room was full of friends and family. We just could not take care of all the people who wanted to hear radio. They came from Hindsville, Siloam Springs, Rogers, and all around just to hear this new marvel. Finally, Dad had an idea. We took out the upstairs attic window and placed the horn speaker so that it aimed outside and downward. Then we borrowed folding chairs to seat fifty people. Sometimes every chair was filled, with some listeners sitting on the grass.

I suppose we could now say radio was off and running. In reality it was more like a slow walk. To understand why, let's take a look at some of the factors involved.

Before 1927 all radios were battery-powered. Only those who remember that time can fully appreciate the cost and problems involved with battery operation. Unlike today's radios, they required more than a tiny dry cell costing less than a dollar. And what a nightmare they were to hook up: two wires to the "A" Battery, usually three to the "B" batteries, and at least two to the "C" battery. In addition, there were connections between each of the "B" batteries. One slip, one wrong connection—and you could blow two months' salary. If you succeeded in getting the batteries connected correctly, you had four more connections to make: one to the antenna, one to ground, and two to the speaker or headphones.

Radio batteries were large, heavy, and expensive. Placed on the floor under the radio table, batteries added little to the decor of the parlor. Lead acid "A" batteries had a nasty habit of eating holes in the carpet and would within time do permanent damage to floors.

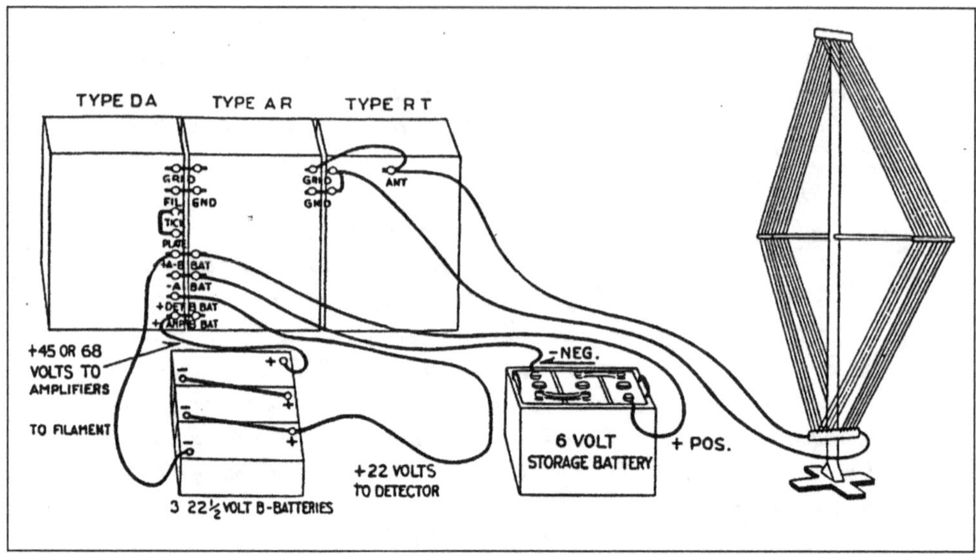

Diagram showing hookup of the Westinghouse RA-DA regenerative receiver. Loop antennas were sometimes used when the installation of an outdoor antenna was impractical. From a 1922 instruction book.

Perhaps the most annoying feature of battery-powered radios was the need to have the "A" battery recharged at regular intervals, usually every two weeks. This involved removal of the battery, a trip to the nearest garage or service station which offered recharging service, and a wait of at least three days while the battery charged. There were no quick-chargers in those days. The fee for charging a battery ranged from fifty to seventy-five cents.

There was no shortage of places where one could have batteries charged. Automotive garages, hardware stores, and even a few enterprising grocers bought chargers. Cost of a heavy duty unit—one that would charge up to a dozen batteries at a time—ran from sixty to eighty dollars.

"B" batteries were of the dry cell type, 45 volts per battery with a 22.5 volt tap or 22.5 volts only. With a listening time of two hours a day, "B" batteries could be expected to last about two months. Cost ran from $1.50 to $1.75 each. The smallest battery required was a low voltage, low amperage "C" battery that furnished bias for the tubes. It cost less than one dollar and lasted a very long time.

More affluent owners purchased two "A" batteries and a charging device. One battery was kept on the charger, while the other was attached to the radio. Cost of battery and charger ran about fifty dollars.

The radio itself would likely employ a regenerative detector. While extremely sensitive, these sets were difficult to tune. Normally, three dials had to be adjusted to the station frequency. Other controls included the cantankerous regeneration adjustment, antenna coupling, filament voltage, and volume controls. If the operator tuned everything correctly, reception on a clear, cold night might include stations from several hundred miles away. More likely, stations within a hundred miles or so would come in through static crashes, noise, and interference from adjacent stations. We are assuming, of course, that an aerial at least one hundred feet long, high, and in the clear, plus a good ground rod, had been properly installed.

Better radios had ample power to drive a horn type loudspeaker; now the entire family could listen at the same time. Speakers were little more than a single headphone attached to a horn made of molded composition, wood, or metal; hence a "tinny" sound was associated with early radio.

What did all this cost? Let's look at a typical magazine ad from this period. In 1922, RCA ran an ad for their Aeriola Grand, a four-tube radio. Complete with mahogany stand, storage battery, battery charger, and antenna wire, the price was $409.95. To better understand the cost of radio, let's see what $409.95 would buy in 1922.

For $400 you could pay tuition for one student at the University of Arkansas for a full four-year education, with money left over. The old Blue Mill Cafe, a few years later, served a 16 oz. sirloin steak with all the trimmings for 80 cents. With $400 you could take a family of four on a two-week vacation to the Grand Canyon and buy trinkets at every Indian trading post along the route. Or perhaps you needed a new car— a Ford or Chevrolet could be purchased for approximately the same cost as the Aeriola.

Yes, radio must come down in price, improve in quality of reception, become easier to operate, and be made into an attractive piece of furniture before it would become a common household accessory.

All this became possible in 1927 with the introduction of AC tubes. Now, radios could be plugged into any electrical outlet—no more messy and expensive batteries. Higher voltages available from AC power supplies meant widespread use of the superheterodyne circuit, single control tuning of frequency, louder reception, better tonal quality, lower prices, and smaller cabinets. Finally, radio was on its way. Even the great depression could not slow the growth of this mighty juggernaut—radio.

> *Radio communication of the future obviously tends to include all moving vehicles; it is already beyond the experimental stage for installation on ships at sea, in submersibles, in aircraft, and railroad trains. It is reasonable to expect its eventual application to automobiles and even in some cases to individuals.*
>
> NEW YORK SUNDAY TIMES, MAY 14, 1922
> DAVID SARNOFF (1891–1971)
> GENERAL MANAGER, RCA

The years from 1927–28 until the start of World War II did not see any radical improvements in broadcast radio. What we did see was a gradual evolution of the art, a steady improvement of basic ideas and construction practices. As a matter of fact, radios built in 1946–50 were generally inferior to those built in 1935. So called improvements like AC-DC tubes, slug tuning, miniature tubes, and modular construction resulted in a less dependable, low fidelity, and costly to maintain product. Later, after years of perfection, some of the ideas would prove practical.

Well-known names from the twenties began to disappear. Atwater Kent, De Forest, Majestic, Freshman, Freed-Eisemann, and dozens more were replaced by companies which would become giants of the radio industry: RCA, Zenith, Magnavox, Crosley, General Electric, Philco, and newcomers Admiral and Motorola.

> *Of all the dramatic media, radio is the most visual.*
> JOHN REEVES
> ENGLISH TENOR

For Americans growing up during the Great Depression, radio was a vital part of life. No other age group would, or could, share their feeling toward this great entertainment medium. The golden era of radio started in the late twenties and ended, rather quickly, in the late forties. Its demise, while expected, caught many of us in the business off guard. It is absolutely unbelievable—so short a life span for such a wonderful invention.

Before 1927 and the introduction of the electric radio, listening time was carefully allotted to a few favorite programs. By the 1940s everyone, including families on a limited budget, could afford to use the radio as much as they pleased.

How much did it cost to operate a electric radio? Well, in 1930 most utility companies charged between three and four cents per kilowatt hour. The average console or floor model radio with six to ten tubes might use eighty watts. Table radios drew somewhere between forty and sixty watts. If my eighth grade arithmetic is correct, a radio pulling sixty watts, at four cents per KWH, would cost around one fourth cent per hour to operate. Large consoles might cost one third cent per hour. Fifteen hours of entertainment for a nickel is a good investment.

If possible, families finished their evening meal around five o'clock. This gave mother enough time to "do" the dishes before joining the family around the radio. The evening's radio listening started with Lowell Thomas and the six o'clock news. Who can ever forget that wonderful voice? It made even cheap radio speakers vibrate with a deep resonance.

"Good evening, Mr. and Mrs. North and South America, and all the ships and clippers at sea! Let's go to press! Flash!" With this well-known line, Walter Winchell opened his evening news broadcasts. His fast delivery and coverage of the more off-beat and sensational news items assured him a large audience. Winchell had a running feud with Ben Bernie. The best of friends, they used the "feud" to garner more listeners to each of their radio programs.

And how we loved *Amos n' Andy!* Sure, they were "colored" and not too good at running the taxi, but we were not laughing at a race—we were laughing at two individuals.

Bob Burns and his bazooka—how we enjoyed his jokes. No one was offended because he was an Arkansan from Van Buren. He was a comedian, and he was funny. Who could take offense if he was from our home state?

Equally popular was *Lum and Abner* from Pine Ridge. Most of us could relate in some way to those two old-timers running the "Jot 'em Down Store." No offense was intended for people in Arkansas, and none taken. Why are people so sensitive today?

And talk about realism—*Death Valley Days* was so real you could smell the odors of the twenty-mule teams and feel the heat of Death Valley.

Smilin' Ed McConnell did much to save the eyesight of America. He was on the air for Aladdin Kerosene Mantle Lamps. Remember—much of our country lived in rural areas not yet serviced by any electric company. Night after night, Smilin' Ed softly and convincingly told farmers across this land that they were ruining the eyesight of their children by not buying an Aladdin lamp. He reminded us of poor Mother, trying to darn socks and piece quilts by the flickering yellow light from our old-fashioned lamp. He told us about Grandma—her eyes no longer strong—and oh, how much she would like to read her Bible again.

And, by gosh, people believed him. "Smilin' Ed" wouldn't mislead you! When a travelling salesman came around selling Aladdin lamps, farm families scraped up the seven to ten dollars needed, so they could listen to the radio in a well-lighted room. You know what—he was right! The Aladdin was well worth the money.

Remember Don Ameche and *First Nighter?* In the 1930s everyone in America was treated to a Broadway show every week. Who needed to see the action? It was just as real as your imagination could make it.

Jack Benny and Rochester, Bob Hope, George Burns and Gracie Allen, Will Rogers, Joe Penner, Fibber McGee and Molly, Red Skelton, Eddie Cantor, Fred Allen (remember *Allen's Alley?*), Jimmy Durante, Ed Wynn, Milton Berle, and Charlie McCarthy, aided by Edgar Bergen, of course, entertained us with jokes and comedy skits—none of which had, or needed, four-letter words.

Two people, President Franklin D. Roosevelt and H. V. Kaltenborn, with their compelling radio personalities, did much to pull America through the Great Depression and the first frightening months of World War II.

President Roosevelt (FDR) and his "fireside chats" could very well have saved this country from a revolution in the early thirties. Millions were unemployed, banks were failing; plants and small businesses were closing. Money just disappeared from circulation.

There were no insured bank accounts, no welfare payments, no food stamps, no unemployment insurance, no Social Security checks, no government help of any kind. If you were out of work, you were out of food. Larger cities opened up soup kitchens to keep people from starving. Those lucky enough to live in the country grew their food.

The country was caught up in strikes, marches on the Capitol—riots, crime, and unrest that could have led us into a revolution. Then FDR came on the radio and told us: "The only thing you have to fear—is fear itself." He assured us the government was going to take action. We were willing to wait and see. As he promised, things began to improve. Progress was slow, but each year was a little better than the preceding one.

Then came Pearl Harbor! We were caught with our pants at half-mast. All the explaining by the military could not cover up the fact that we were terribly unprepared to fight a war—a war raging on two sides of us. In the Atlantic our ships were being sunk by German U-boats every week. France had fallen. Russia was being beaten back. England was hanging on by sheer guts alone. We lost base after base in the Pacific, including the Philippines. The loss of American lives was staggering—Wake Island, Bataan, Corregidor. It seemed there was nothing but bad news; there was no hope.

Then we turned on the radio for Gabriel Heatter's news broadcast. "Ah, yes, there's good news tonight," Mr. Heatter would say. Then he would stress the good news that had happened that day. It might be insignificant to the rest of the world, but it was encouraging to hear just a little bit of good news. Somehow we always slept a little better after listening to Gabriel Heatter.

Remember those great "remotes" we used to listen to after going to bed? You could close your eyes and go to ballrooms from coast to coast: The Meadowbrook, The Rustic Cabin, The Paragon, Roseland, The Coconut Grove, The Pump Room, The Glen Island Casino—one after the other until we finally went to sleep. And the bands—Rudy Vallee, Kaye Kyser, Blue Barron, Herbie Kaye, Sammy Kaye, Bob Chester, Jack Teagarden, Artie Shaw, The Dorseys, Bob Crosby, Glenn Miller, Benny Goodman, Chick Webb, Count Basie, Jimmy Lunceford, Jay McShann, Larry Clinton, Glen Gray, Ben Bernie, Ted Lewis, and yes, even Lawrence Welk, though I never met anyone when I was young who liked his music. Lawrence Welk's music was like oatmeal; most people developed a taste for it about the time their teeth fell out.

Just for fun, let's take a little test. Match up the words on the right with the band leaders on the left.

1.	Ted Lewis	A. The Dipsy Doodler
2.	Ben Bernie	B. The Casa Loma Orchestra
3.	Rudy Vallee	C. Swing and Sway with____________
4.	Benny Goodman	D. The Bobcats
5.	Artie Shaw	E. A megaphone
6.	Sammy Kaye	F. Is Everybody Happy?
7.	Lawrence Welk	G. The Old Maestro
8.	Bob Crosby	H. The King of Swing
9.	Glen Gray	I. The Champagne Music of____________
10.	Larry Clinton	J. The Gramercy Five

If you missed one or two answers, ask some old-timer or look up the answers at the end of this chapter.

Advancement of vacuum tube technology enabled rural families to enjoy radio almost as economically as their city cousins. Shortly after the introduction of electric radios, manufacturers developed two-volt radio tubes. The "thousand hour" battery pack was born soon after. One battery, one plug to connect to the battery, and you were ready to enjoy one thousand hours of entertainment. Within a few years battery life was extended to 1,300 hours. The cost was about five dollars; total cost of listening, not much more than for those living in the cities.

Did anyone play records in those pre-war years? Sure they did, but not to any great extent. Juke box operators accounted for much of the record market. Recorded music technology was on hold.

Ten-inch 78 RPM records, unchanged since 1914, were still the industry standard. They played less than four minutes per side. Some 12-inch records were available—mostly classical music. Playing time for this larger record was about five minutes.

Records were played on one of three types of machines: the old wind-up phonograph, cheap portable phonographs, and radio-phonograph combinations. It was well-known that every time a record was played on a wind-up phonograph, the record suffered considerable damage. Sharp steel needles, plus a heavy pickup pressure, quickly destroyed what little fidelity the record possessed in the beginning. A surface noise or scratchy sound was superimposed on the music in the delicate record grooves after very few playings.

I remember buying a few 78s from Guisinger's Music House in Fayetteville during my college years. They cost me seventy-five cents in 1940. Few jobs were available that paid over thirty-five cents per hour. It took two hours labor to buy three minutes of recorded music. Little effort was spent by recording companies to offer true high fidelity recordings. The public had not been educated to appreciate good sound, and those who did were likely to own equipment incapable of reproducing wide-range recordings.

Electric phonographs and radio-phonograph combinations used electrical pickups; most weighed in excess of twenty-five grams. Piezo-electric, or crystal pickups, common throughout the industry, required a heavy stylus pressure for proper operation. Demand for high quality record playing equipment did not warrant large expenditures of capital by manufacturers.

Music lovers became aware of potential record damage early on and resorted to many devices to minimize record wear. One of the more successful was use of cactus needles. Cactus did much less damage to the delicate records and imparted a softness to reproduced sound that many found pleasing. A cactus needle, if it was to sound its best, required sharpening after every record—a lot of trouble for three minutes of music. Cactus needle sharpeners, available for around two dollars, made the chore a little less unpleasant.

Others, like me, rigged up a counterweight to lessen needle pressure. My records lasted longer; however, fidelity suffered when crystal pickups were operated at less than the recommended stylus pressure.

Steel needles came in small envelopes. A dozen or so cost twenty-five cents. Cactus needles cost a little more. "Permanent" style needles with either sapphire or diamond points became available before World War II. Costing from $1.50 to $5, they sold well, even though record wear was accelerated by their use.

To overcome the inconvenience of changing records every three minutes, most companies offered record-changers. "Record destroyers" would have been a more appropriate name. When they worked, which was only occasionally, your records were scratched and chipped. If you forgot and left records on the changer, they tended to warp, especially in warm weather. It is easy to understand why consumers were reluctant to spend hard-earned dollars on phonograph records.

As early as 1860, Paul Nipkow of Germany designed a simple disc; around the outer edge was a spiral of holes containing small lenses. Its purpose was to transmit pictures through a wire. Later the disc was combined with wireless to send pictures through the air. Various mechanical means of transmitting pictures were developed by others before the turn of the century. Some produced pictures good enough to encourage further experimentation. None compared, however, to the Zworykin iconoscope—a modification of the cathode ray tube.

In 1926, John Logie Baird demonstrated his television system to the Royal Institute in London. This system, unfortunately, still relied on the Nipkow mechanical system of TV. Though the British Broadcasting Company was impressed, they finally realized that, if TV was to become practical, the mechanical systems must be replaced by more modern technology. They started broadcasting in 1934 with the Zworykin system, using an iconoscope in the camera and a cathode ray tube in the receiver. These TV transmissions were far superior to the disc. The results were sharp black-and-white images with a good gray scale, whereas the disc television produced silhouette-type pictures only. Though the disc was inferior to electronic scanning, a few still believed in the obsolete mechanical TV system. Amateur experimenters were especially fond of scanning disc TV, because it contained few parts and was easy to build. And the cost was a small fraction of cathode ray systems.

Strangely enough, today in 1994, scanning disc TV kits are still manufactured for sale to schools, museums, and radio experimenters interested in antique equipment.

Television was demonstrated to millions during the New York World's Fair in 1939. Images had a greenish-blue cast and were limited to postcard size, but millions who watched the small pictures came away convinced TV would soon be in every home. A few television stations, financed by various manufacturers, transmitted television images occasionally during the 1930s, some on a rather loose weekly schedule.

By the end of World War II, necessary technology was in place to build television transmitting stations and receiving sets. There was a general feeling among the buying public that TV was at last just around the corner.

We must make decisions and predictions based upon present day technology. If the general public had understood the magnitude of the problems that faced the TV industry, they would have been less optimistic. Those in the industry were aware of problems the public never even thought of—and some seemed impossible to solve. To us, TV was "down the road a piece," not "around the corner."

For example, if coast to coast TV was to become a reality, there must be a method of connecting every TV station in America to network studios. Otherwise, our TV programs would be limited to film or live programs produced in each TV station studio. The obvious solution was to run a very expensive, low loss, high definition co-axial cable to every TV station. Cost was estimated in the many billions of dollars. Completion time—about twenty years.

Who could dream that when the Russians launched the little beep-beeping Sputnik that our problems were practically solved? Communication satellites could do the job of the cable—much better and at a fraction of the cost.

Answers to quiz: 1-F, 2-G, 3-E, 4-H, 5-J, 6-C, 7-I, 8-D, 9-B, 10-A

PEOPLE AND PLACES INDEX

BUSINESS INDEX

NAME OF FIRM	MAP	BLDG	OWNER(S)
Acme Electric	4	63	Albert Hough
Allard, Clyde—radio service	4	93E	Clyde Allard
American Beauty Shop	4	84A	Goldie England
Apollo Theater	2	11	Bill Sonneman
Applegate's Drug Store	3	39	Tim Applegate
Arkansas Brokerage	3	33	Garvin Martini
Arkansas Western Gas Company	3	49	Vol Lester—manager
Austin Mercantile	2	16	
Barber Shop (Name?)	5	101	
Bargain Center	4	96	Garvin Martini
Barrack's Antiques Gallery	4	61	Dallas Barrack
Barrack's Grocery	3	30	Jim Barrack
Beddingfield Shoe Shop	7	125	Louis Beddingfield
Blue Castle Tavern	4	74	Ray and Monica Kuester
Bon-Ton Cleaners	4	79	Tom Warren until early 1950s; then Bob Godbold
Brogdon and Hazel	6	109	Forrest Hazel and Paul Brogdon
Brogdon Spray Supplies	6	113	Byron Brogdon sold to Dan Ingrum in 1950s.
Brown, Jeff D.—poultry lab	6	111	Jeff D. Brown
Brown, Jeff D.—feed mill	5	106	Jeff D. Brown
Brown, Jeff D.—offices and hatchery	6	114	Jeff D. Brown
Bruce's Electric Shop (1946–47)	5	104	Bruce Vaughan
Bruce's Electric Shop (1947–50)	4	76	Bruce Vaughan
Bruce's Radio and TV (1950–55)	5	99E	Bruce Vaughan
			On Sept. 1, 1955, Bruce's moved into its own building at 1125 South Thompson (Highway 71).
Burt, Leo and Ruth—furniture	2	14	Leo and Ruth Burt
Bus Station—Trailways	2	19	Tom Keith, manager
Byars Milling Co.	3	26	Leo Byars (?)
Cab Stand (also newsstand)	4	83	Cliff and Jewell Dameron
Cab Stand (newsstand) 1945–49	4	77	Cliff and Jewell Dameron
Callison-Riggs Funeral Home	1	3	Glenn Riggs
Callison-Russell Funeral Home	1	3	Maurice Russell, later Callison-Sisco; then Sisco Funeral Chapel—Gilbert Sisco

the "Chicken Little" on south 71, about one block north of the Worthen Bank Drive-In.

NOT SHOWN ON MAPS:

Dr. Howard Henry—dentist. 212 S. Main Street.

Ray Tabor—blacksmith. South of Emma 1 block, on east side of creek.

Alvin Hotel—operator, Mrs. Lillian Holt. 200 Holcomb Street.

Southern Hotel—operators, Mr. and Mrs. Rice. 214 S. Main, located on site of present Arts Center of the Ozarks. Out of business in mid-1940s.

Pool Parlor—After 1950 when old Opera house burned, Cline Lane built a pool parlor east of his home on the corner of Holcomb and Meadow. Later the house was torn down and replaced by offices.

The bus station was located in the Barnsdall gasoline station on the southeast corner of Emma Avenue and Main Street, 1930s.

Shiloh Museum of Ozark History—Gallery and offices (1991), the Searcy House (1870s), the Ritter cabin (1854), Dr. Carter's Office (1880s), and General Store (1870s). Located on north side of Johnson Avenue, extending from North Main Street to Spring Creek (Town Branch). The Gregg house, originally between the museum and the Searcy House, has been moved. The home of Bell and Lottie Phillips, located behind the Gregg house, was moved also.

INDEX BY BUILDING NUMBER

The nine plates that follow on pages 128–136 were adapted from the 1948 series of Sanborn Fire Insurance Maps. Insurance companies used such maps to help them set rates. Springdale was mapped in 1897, 1904, 1909, 1914, 1924, and 1948. The Shiloh Museum of Ozark History has copies of all of these maps made from originals held by the Special Collections Division of the University of Arkansas Libraries.

BUILDING NUMBER	MAP NUMBER	BUSINESS FIRM
1	1	Claypool—residence
2	1	Deaver, Frank—residence
2A	1	Hunt, Bill—residence
2B	1	Parke Avalon Studio after Opera House burned; erected 1950–51
2C	1	Watts, D. C., Electric—after 1950
2R	1	Fitzgerald, Ewell—residence
3	1	Callison-Riggs Funeral Home, later Callison-Russell, now (1994) Sisco Funeral Chapel
4	1	Gaskin Grocery—Allen Gaskin
5	1	Redwine, Joe—residence. Since 1949–50, Sisco Clinic
6	1	Rush-Guise Restaurant. Delores Beauty Shop, early 1950s
7	1	Griggs Grocery—Tolbert Griggs
8	1	Jones Recapping
9	2	Ozark Motor Company (Hudson dealership—B. J. Hainbach, owner)
10	1	Rush-Guise duplex
11	2	Apollo Theater, late 1940s
12	2	Francisco, Loyd—apartments
13	2	Furry—residence
14	2	Clark & Eoff Furniture. Sold in early 1950s to Leo Burt. Clark and Eoff moved to temporary quarters (probably #28) before move to new store at Hwy. 71 and Sunset
15	2	Stout-Condra Automotive Supply
15B	2	Stout-Condra Electric & Motor Service, in basement
16	2	Austin Mercantile and Grocery
17	2	Loyd's Shoe Shop
18	2	Springdale Post Office

TRIVIA

Quandt Street, a muddy, infrequently travelled street, was known as Lovers Lane (with adequate justification) before WWII. The name Quandt Street was unknown to most residents.

———

The stretch of highway from Jones Truck Lines to the turn at East Mountain was known as "The Long Lane." It was a favorite stretch of road to test the speed of a car.

———

The little abandoned building at the intersection of Monitor Road and East Emma (412 Alt.) is the old Becker Machine Shop. James Becker and his father ran the shop for years; it was one of the first machine shops in the area.

———

Stobaugh's store and filling station was located on East Emma at the northwest corner of the airport, now the rodeo grounds.

———

Building #70, owned by the Zimmerman sisters, was used by Joe Nix as a combination undertaking and paint/wallpaper store. He usually displayed two or three coffins in the wallpaper area. Many coffins were actually built in the building.

———

John and Gertrude Welch retired from their garage business after WWII and bought a farm east of Springdale. They took in a young man named Carl Collins to help on their farm. He killed John outside the home; he attacked Gertrude inside the house and left her for dead, but she wrote "Carl killed us" in blood on the kitchen floor. She survived and testified at the trial of Collins, who had been captured out of state. He was convicted, given the death penalty and later executed.

———

The Famous Hardware Company had one of the first gas pumps in Springdale. A single hand-operated pump and an air hose were available on the sidewalk alongside the hardware store. All went well until the "pop-off" valve on the air compressor failed to function. The air tank exploded with a mighty force, blowing a large hole in the side of the establishment. This ended their gas service. *Source—Robert "Bob" H. Clark, son of The Famous Hardware Company founder.*

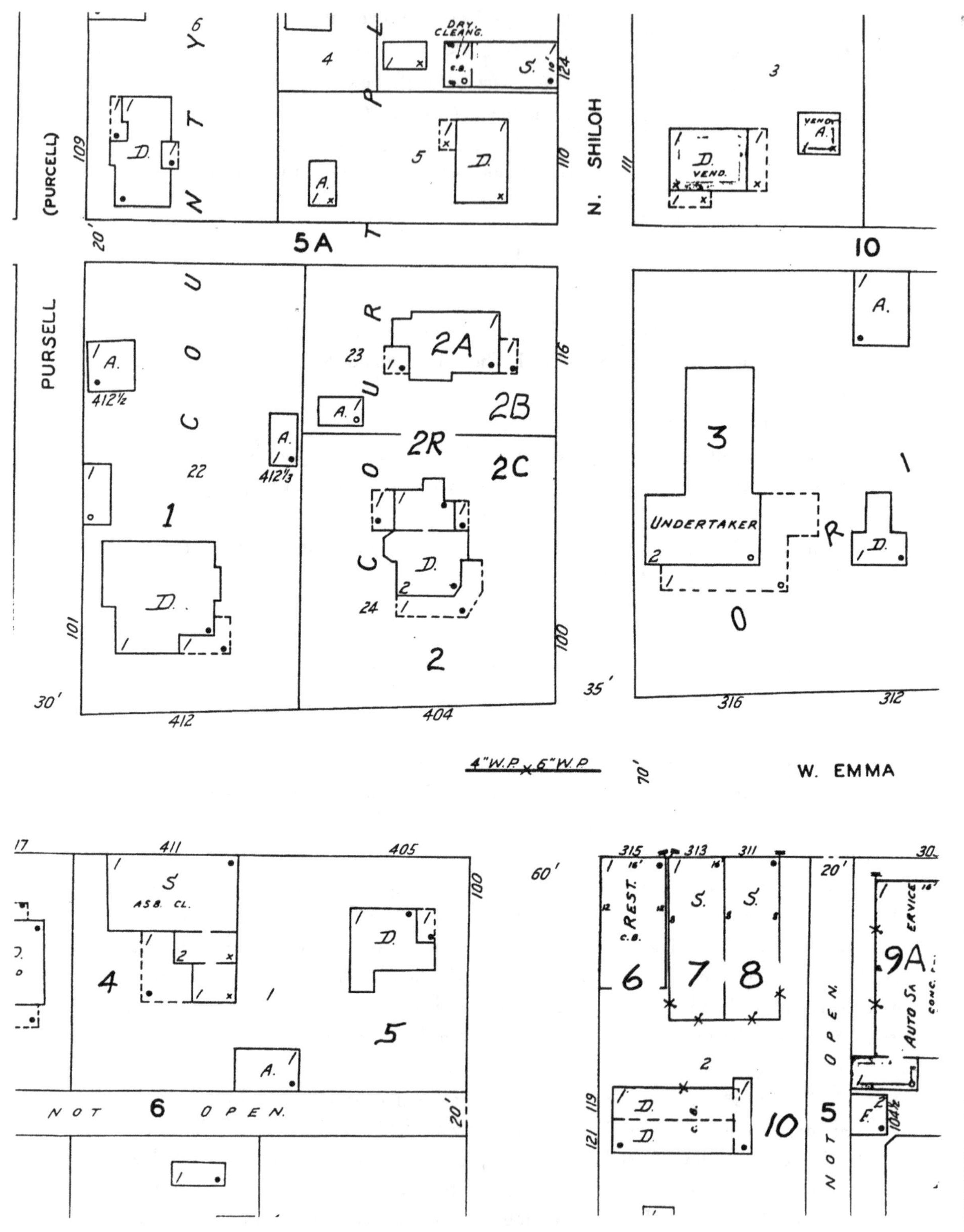

Emma Avenue, 1947, Plate 1

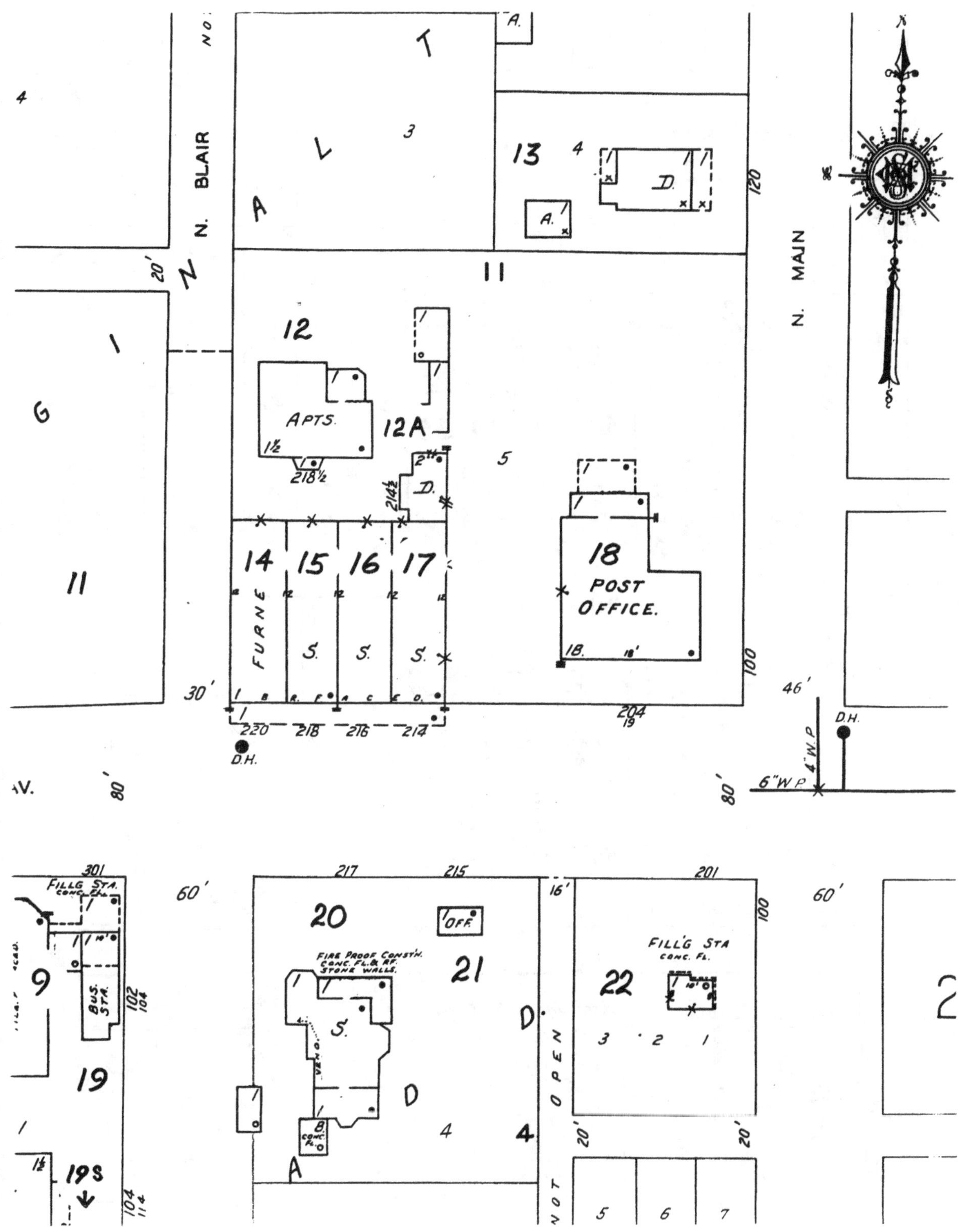

Emma Avenue, 1947, Plate 2

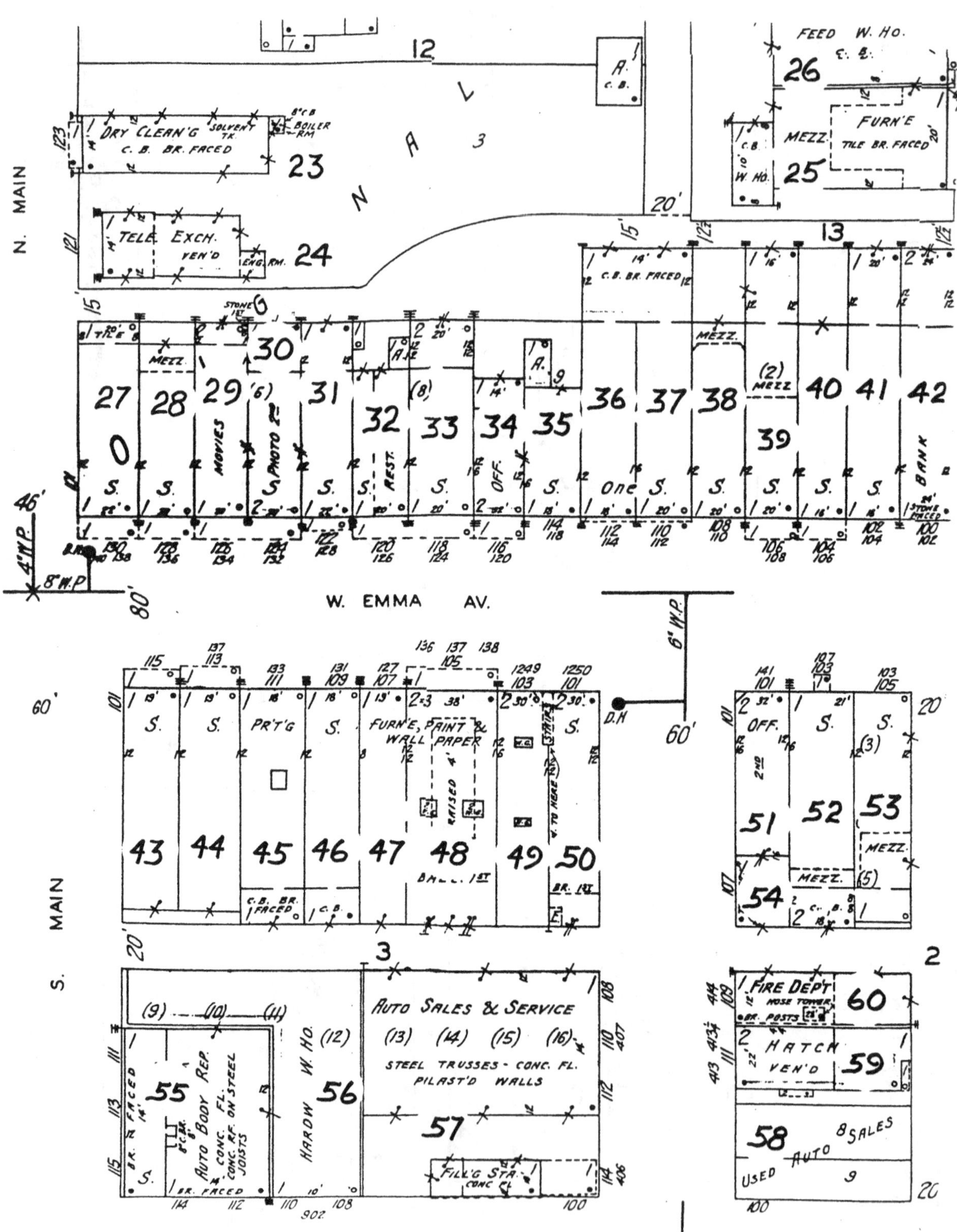

Emma Avenue, 1947, Plate 3

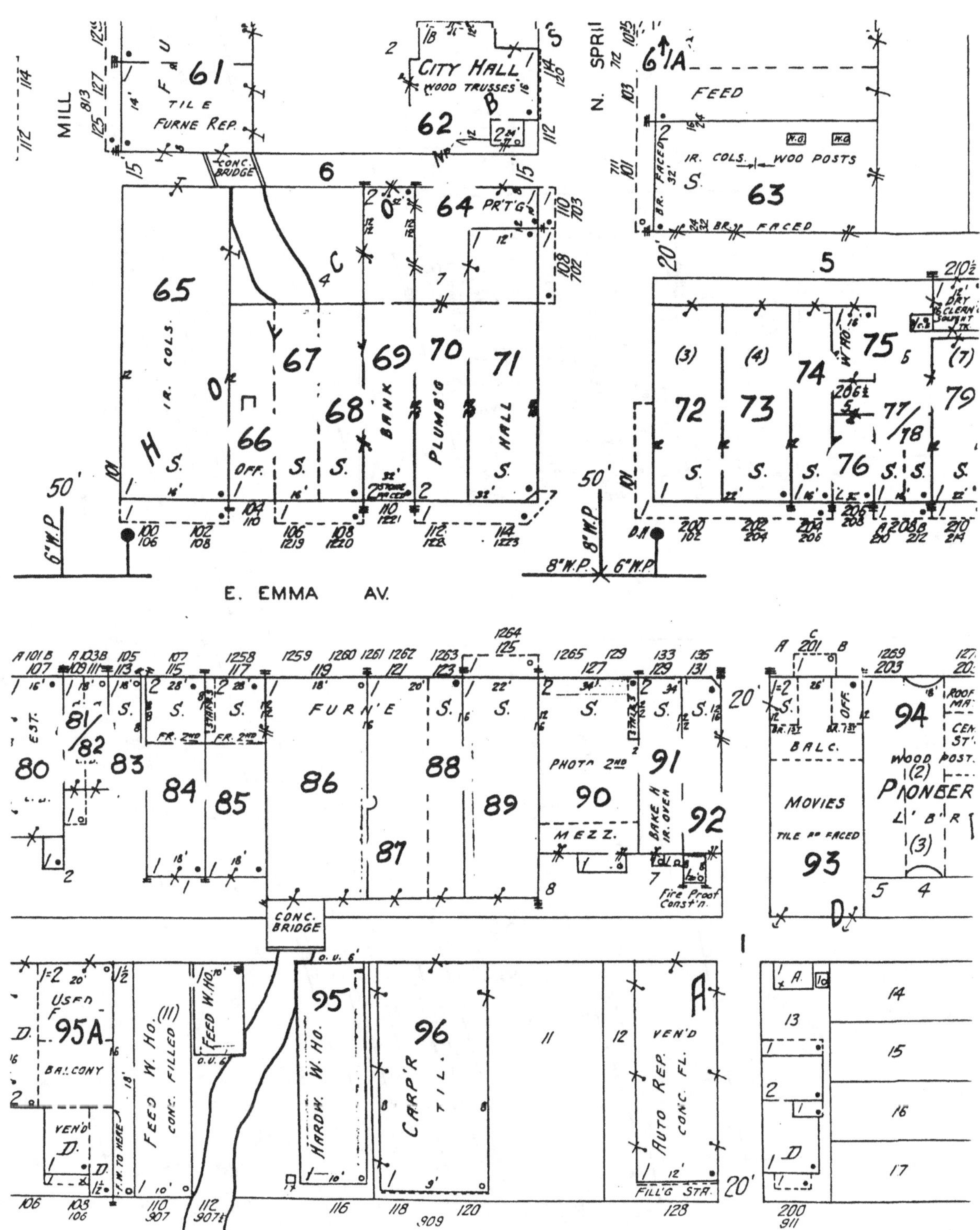

Emma Avenue, 1947, Plate 4

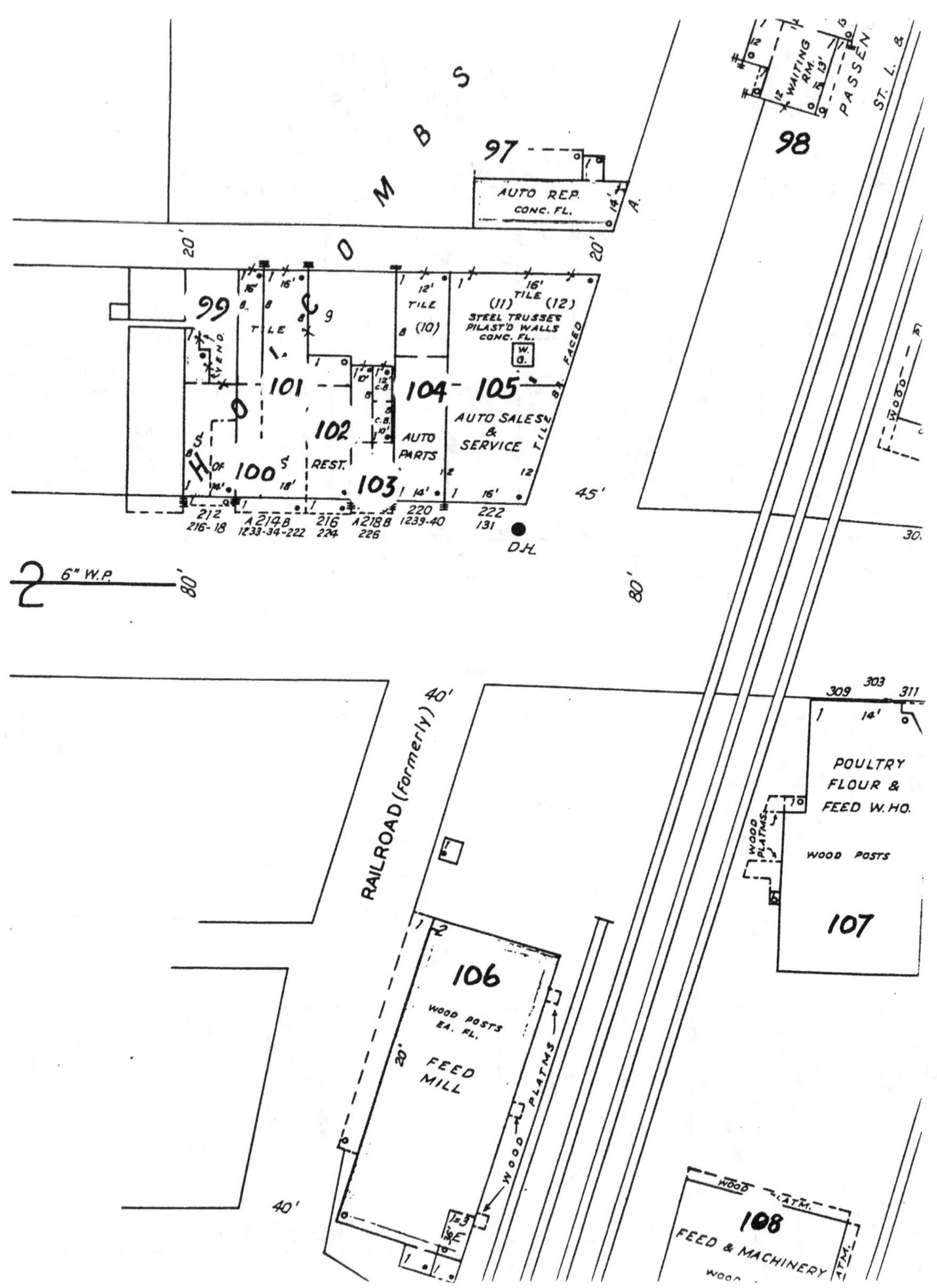

Emma Avenue, 1947, Plate 5

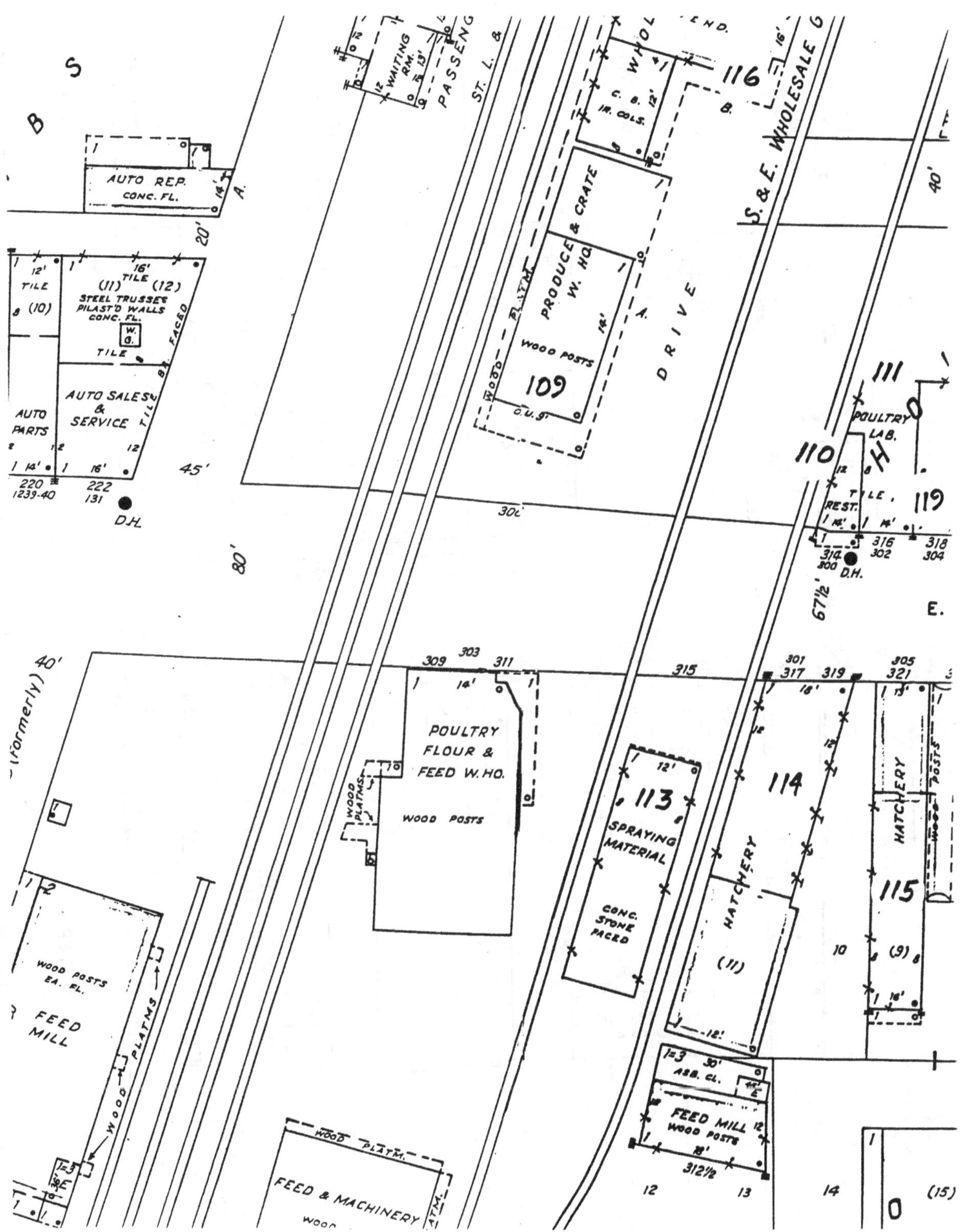

Emma Avenue, 1947, Plate 6

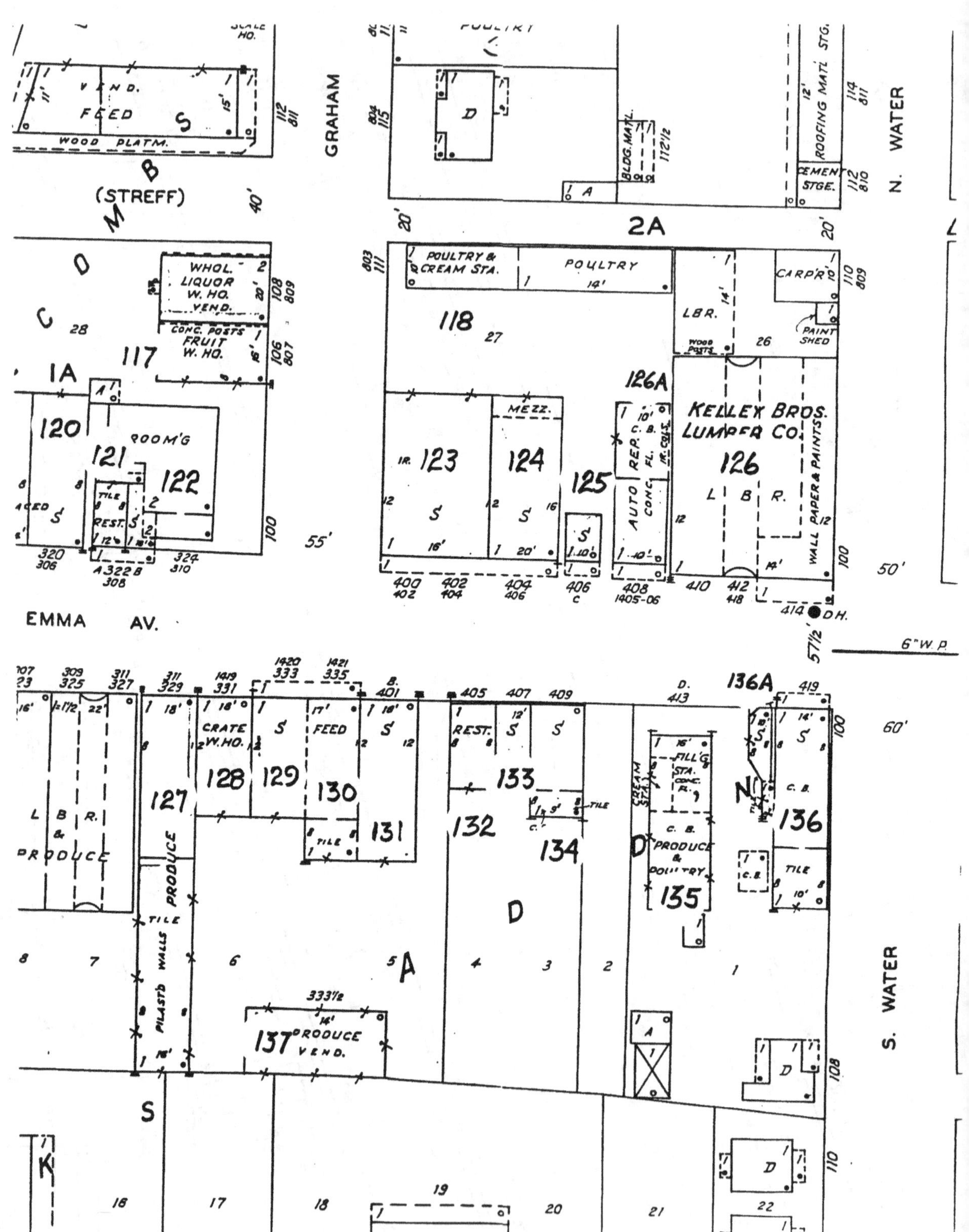

Emma Avenue, 1947, Plate 7

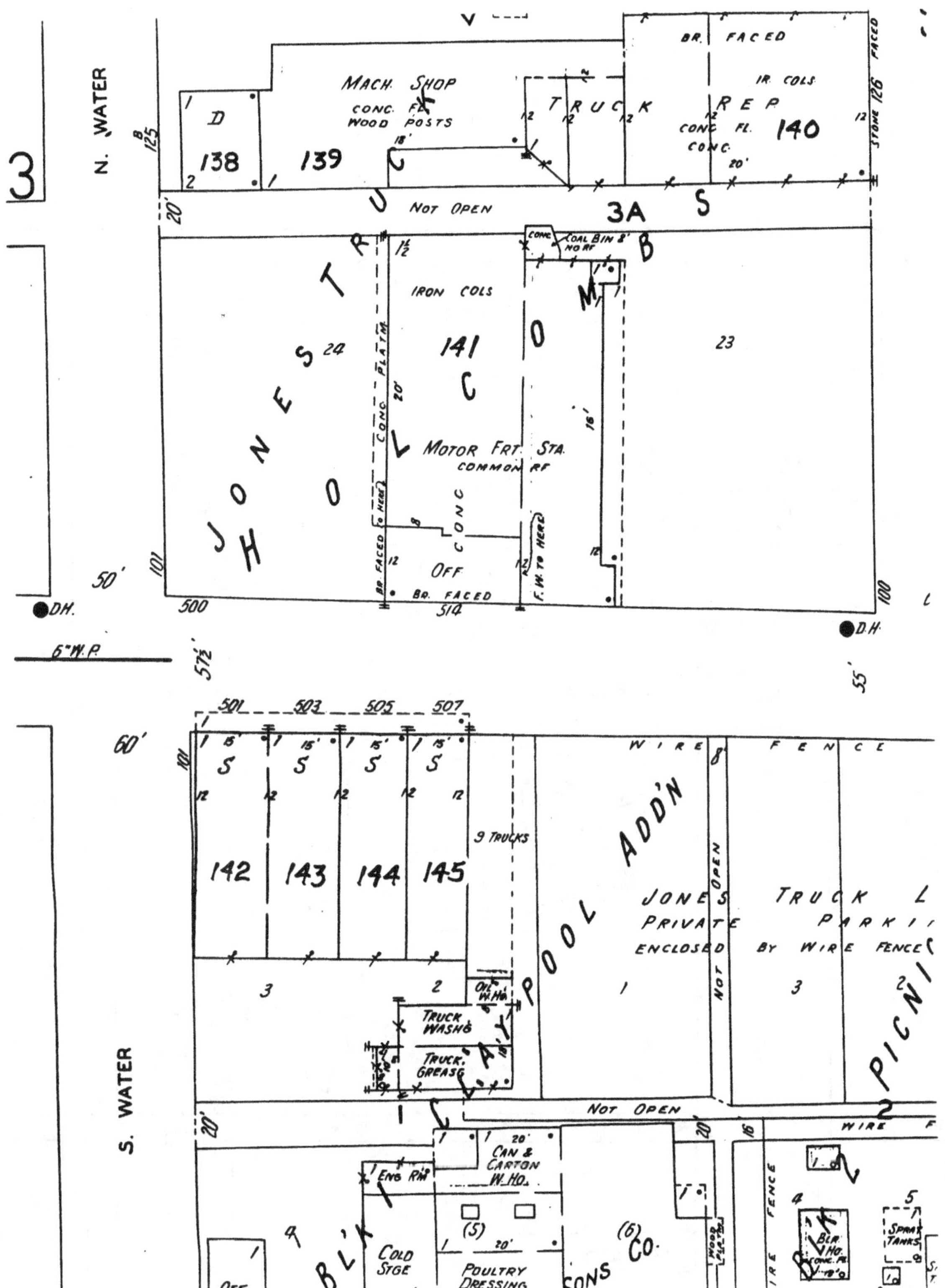

Emma Avenue, 1947, Plate 8

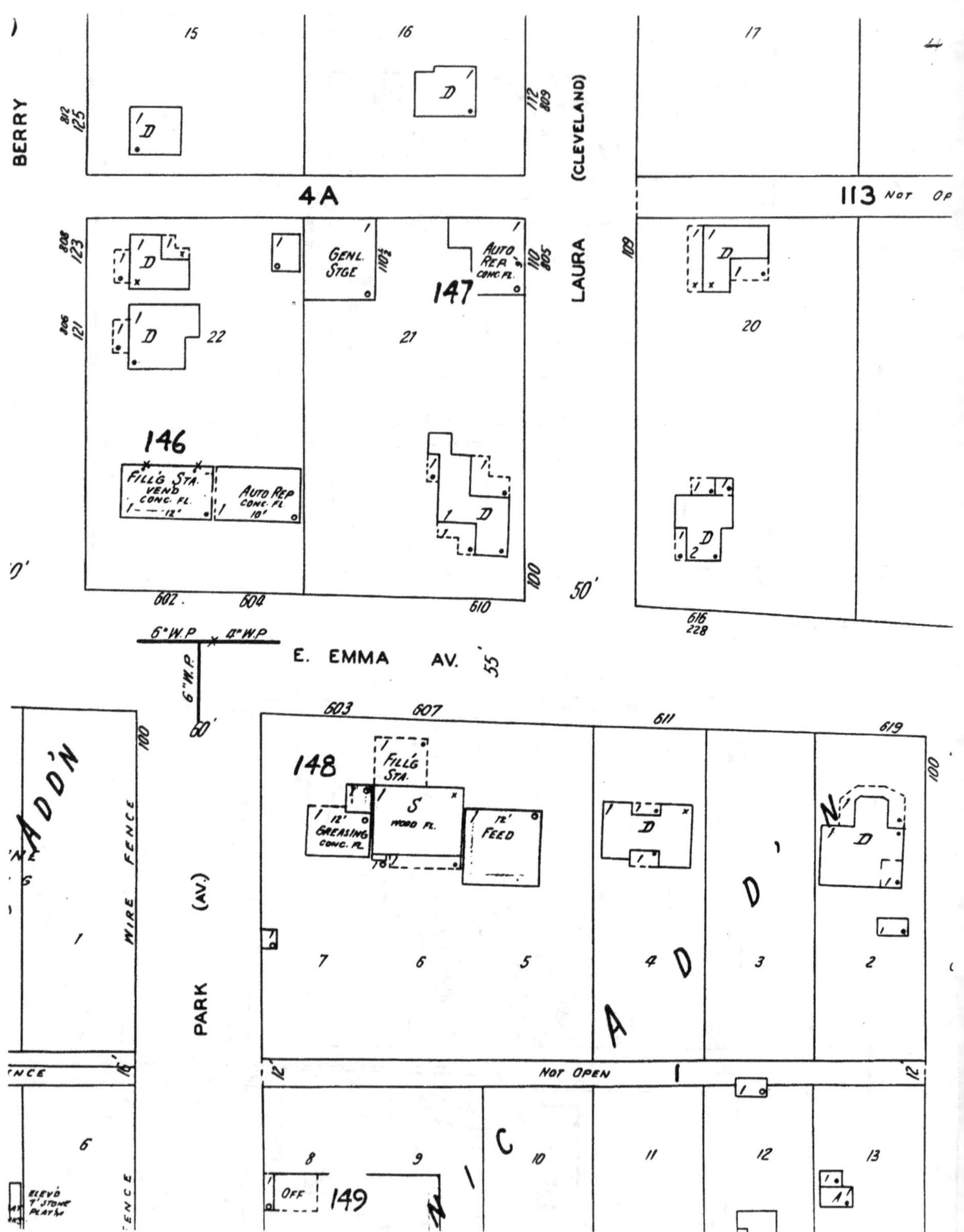

Emma Avenue, 1947, Plate 9

'Snow' May Sift Through Screen; Television Wonderful Just the Same

By THE RAMBLER

The wonders of television are hard to believe.

You sit right there in the front room and see what is going on in a studio hundreds of miles away. It's true. there's no doubt about it. Yet. you come away with disbelief. You marvel at the minds which have made television—the latest modern miracle—a reality. and not just a dreamed-up fantasy described in some pulp scientific magazine.

Bruce Vaughn. Jr. called on the telephone and said:

"Come on over, Oklahoma City's coming in pretty plain now and I believe you can get a good show."

We hurried to the Vaughan home on Allen street. Going into the back room where the 30-tube television set was in operation, we first spotted the big antenna which is anchored on a three-foot-deep concrete pier in the back yard.

Of triangular construction. the tower plus its stacked array aerial reaches 65 feet into the air. Because normal television range is restricted within a 30-mile radius of the transmitter, it is imperative to have a very high aerial in order to receive programs when the set owner lives considerable distance from the station.

The tower is of triangular design, made of spring steel tubing. It has great strength and since it is set in solid concrete. Bruce explained that the guy wires which reach out in four directions from the top are actually not too necessary.

As we entered the room. the big square boxy looking set was receiving a "live talent" program from WKY-TV in Oklahoma City. It was a musical program in which children are invited to participate. Following this, the studio presented a 15-minute cartoon strip which is similar to black-and-white cartoons seen in theaters. After the cartoon, we witnessed. the fourth chapter of a rootin' tootin' serial. with cops and robbers and stuff like that.

After viewing the entertainment for an hour or so it soon becomes evident that a great deal of the programs are beamed for children audiences. We were listening, and watching of course, from 7 to 8:30 p. m. a period in the day when the younsters are beginning to let down somewhat from the day's adventures (so the parents hope). Television should afford a perfect medium to make the kids settle down and relax. It is an utterly fascinating and compelling thing. The only drawback is the fact that once started, the average boy or girl will have to be dragged away from the set with log chains or tow rope.

Normally, better reception from the Oklahoma station is found after a rain storm, Bruce said. Often a fairly low hanging cloud layer will aid reception. Since transmitters send on a straight line, curvature of the earth obstructs the impulses which carry the visual part of the program. The layers of clouds often deflect the waves down, whereas they would usually continue their straight line off into space.

Last night Bruce's set was plagued by a station at Washington. D. C., which sends on channel four the same as WKY-TV The image from Washington was too faint to be seen but it played heck at times with Oklahoma City. Snow on the screen because of electrical interference. distance and weather conditions is one of the worst handicaps to long-range reception. It consists of agitated white particles which flicker and jump and run through the screen, and it does resemble a real snow storm.

Let's take a brief look at the television set itself. Bruce's is straight television. There are also television-radio and television-radio - phonograph combinations available in the highest price brackets. Atop the big receiver are two boosters, which are required when the set is outside the 30-mile limit. Only one was in use last night. The 10-inch screen, which is considered "standard" on present day models, receives the images from the kinescope, a cathode-ray type tube, which, of course, is the heart of any television set. The kinescope is a tube with pressure on the glass of two tons per square inch because of the tremedous vacuum therein.

The image is seen through a heavy glass window which protects the tube. Scanning the end of the kinescope with 525 lines produces the picture, much as half-tone engravings are produced for printing in your Springdale News.

Controls of the receiver are impressive. but simple. There is a large knob on the extreme right hand side, to control which channel is to be used. At the present time there are 13 channels allocated by the FCC. Only one. channel four at Oklahoma City can be considered for daily use at Springdale. Behind the large channel control is a smaller one for more definite tuning.

Below and to the left of the main knob are four others. They are: sound balance, horizonal hold (to stabilize the picture), brightness and contrast.

It doesn't require an engineering degree to operate a television set. It is not as simple as a radio. naturally, but once the function of each control is learned, it becomes an easy matter.

Round-the-clock programs are available in New York City, where all 13 channels are in use. In Southern California, set owners may listen (and watch) from noon to midnight. If the proposed station in Tulsa can get its tower troubles settled, there is a chance that it will be in operation before 1949 has run its course. Applications for stations now under consideration by the FCC include 31 in the state of Arkansas. These will probably use the film strip type of programs, since the expense of outfitting a studio with equipment for handling live talent is great.

Station WKY-TV has the tallest antenna in the United States—988 feet high. This outstanding height is one reason Bruce has such good success in picking up his programs.

"I really believe Springdale is in a good location for television," he said. "I don't know if it is because we are on a plateau or what. but reception here will be very good."

Programs featuring entertainment which originates in studios come in clearer than do serials. cartoons and other film strips. Mrs. Vaughan suggested we turn around and watch the goings-on in the mirror. We did and the screen was much plainer, possibly because it gave an illusion of greater depth.

When a radio station has trouble and the regular program is interrupted, it is the custom to bring in transcribed music to fill the interim before adjustments are made.

On television. Bruce explained. a cartoon is flashed on the screen. It shows an engineer buried deep in the innards of equipment, tearing his hair and tossing tubes right and left, with a statement underneath explaining that technical difficulties have arisen.

Television, video; telesee. look'-n' listen—whatever you might call it.

It's a wonderful thing.

Ellis Stafford had expressed interest in writing a story for *The Springdale News* about this new-fangled medium of home entertainment. I waited several days to get an acceptable picture on my TV. When the reception was good and clear, I called him. As luck would have it, by the time he arrived it was marginal. Nevertheless, he published the above article in July 1949.

Hear the difference!

A loudspeaker is a critical thing. Any vibration in the horn adds sounds that nature never gave to the speaker's voice. And limited range thins down the tone to flat, unreal quality. Some people think that a near-real voice is the best that radio can give ... but not after they have heard a Radiola Loudspeaker!

The difference is the result of elaborate experiment and extended scientific study. The Radiola Loudspeaker has an extraordinary range—gets the full richness of tone. And it adds no sound of its own. To know how clear—how mellow—how *real* your music can be—ask to hear a Radiola Loudspeaker.

Radiola Loudspeaker
Type UZ-1325
Now $25.00

This symbol of quality  RCA is your protection

Radiola
REG. U. S. PAT. OFF.

LOUD SPEAKER

RADIO CORPORATION
OF AMERICA
Sales Offices:
233 Broadway, New York
10 So. La Salle St., Chicago, Ill.
28 Geary St., San Francisco, Cal.

Horn-type speakers enjoyed a brief life span. Coming into prominence in the early 1920s, they were replaced by cone-type speakers before 1903. Their small earphone-type metal diaphragm was no match for 10- or 12-inch paper cones.

Once the 78 RPM disc type records replaced the old cylinder Edison records, sales of records and phonographs soared. It was a rare home in the WWI era that did not own some sort of a phonograph.

The Victor Talking Machine Company later became known as RCA Victor—or more commonly as RCA. It was so aggressive in marketing the phonograph that the name "Victrola" became synonymous with phonograph.

Manufacturers, aware of America's love affair with the automobile, quickly introduced products to satisfy this lucrative market.

One of the major problems that had to be conquered was that of ignition or spark plug noise.

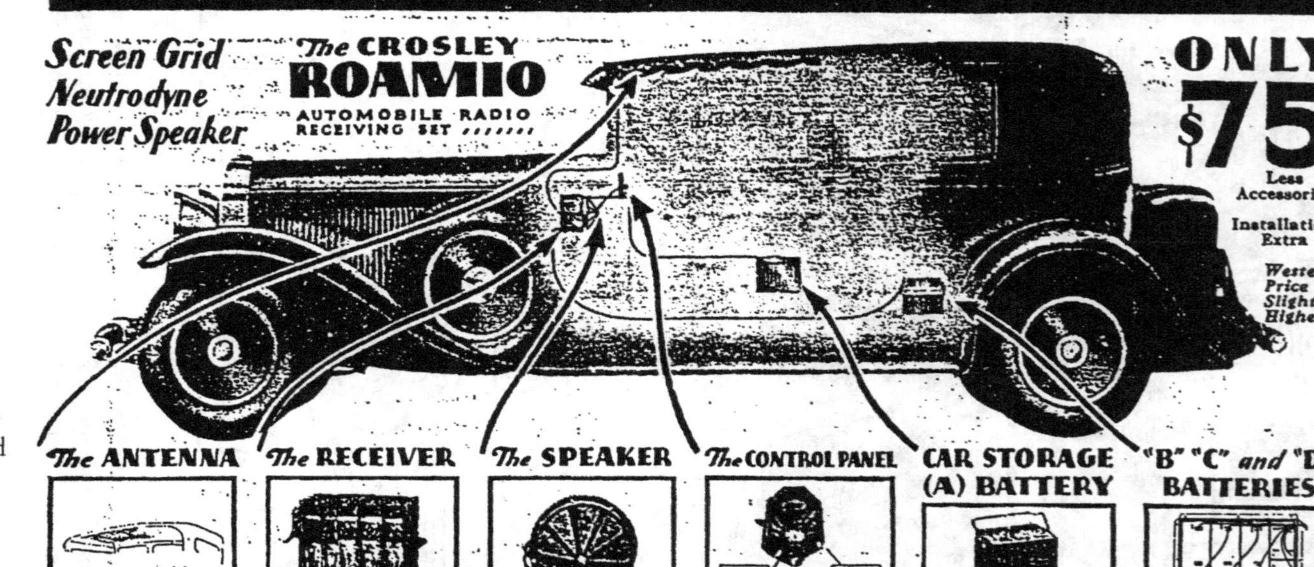

Motorola, a Chicago company, soon dominated the retro-fit market. By stocking four radios, three antennas, and twenty-four control heads, it was possible to fit almost all cars.

In retrospect, the apogee of AM broadcast radio receivers was undoubtedly reached in the mid-1930s. These names were most important: the Zentih Stratosphere, the Scott Philharmonic, and the famous McMurdo Silver Masterpiece.

Carefully designed, they were engineered for the fortunate few who could afford such luxury. Parts were heavily chrome plated; capacitors (condensors) were designed for a long life. The audio output volume and tonal quality was comparable to the finest units in large theaters and auditoriums.

All the engineering and craftsmanship was often hidden from view in a cabinet of fine wood, built by a skilled craftsman. Such sets sold for a price about equal to that of a luxury sedan. Today, if you can find one, the price will be staggering. Radios of this caliber were never manufactured after 1941.

What will your wheat bring?

What will your corn bring? Your livestock? Will it be top price? It will, if you keep in touch with the market—with a RADIOLA.

Practical, dependable and economical is the new RADIOLA III-A. It is achieving distance records greater than sets at far beyond its price—getting cross-country reception with its four tubes. Every word comes in clear and true—music and fun from far away sound as real as if they were in the room. It is the set for the farmer who wants to guide his day's work by the weather reports—guide his marketing by the crop reports—entertain his evenings with good music.

"There's a Radiola for every purse"

Radio Corporation of America
Sales Offices:
233 Broadway, New York City   10 So. La Salle St., Chicago, Ill.
433 California Street, San Francisco, Cal.

Radiola
REG. U.S PAT. OFF.

In this RCA ad, an attempt was made to convince the rural buyer that owning a radio was a necessity. This ploy was used by Henry Ford in marketing the Model T and it worked very well.

For this Broadcasting Receiver thousands have been waiting

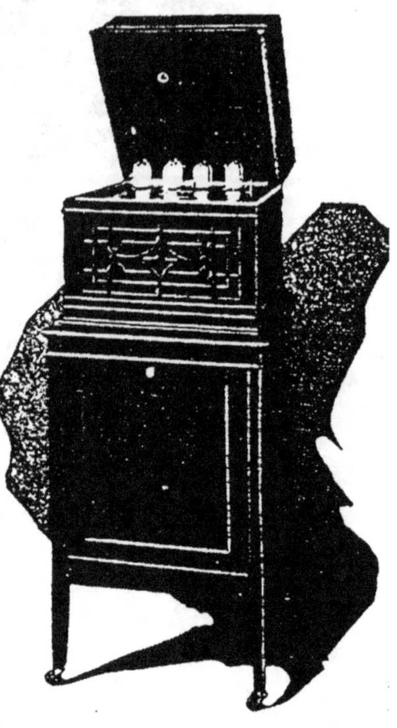

*E*VER since broadcasting became the vogue there has been a demand for a receiver which would fill a whole room with music of perfect tone quality but which would be so simple that anyone could tune in by moving a single lever.

This ideal has at last been realized in the Aeriola Grand—the supreme achievement of present-day radio.

When you hear the voice and the music that come from the Aeriola Grand it is as if the lecturer or singer at the broadcasting station were in your presence. The whole family listens and marvels.

The Aeriola Grand stands unrivaled not only as a radio receiver but as a piece of cabinet work.

Prices

Complete with mahogany stand, storage battery, battery charger, antenna equipment and all accessories $409.50

Without stand, storage battery, charger and receiving antenna equipment $325.00

With stand, but without storage battery, charger and antenna. $350.00

Mahogany stand only . . . . $ 35.00

See the Aeriola Grand at your nearest dealer

Before you buy any receiver, secure a copy of the book "Radio Enters the Home." It tells the real story of radio and will help you to get the most out of this new art. 128 pages—over 200 illustrations—35c a copy. At your dealer or write direct to

What the guests heard at the *Jacksons' Aeriola Grand Party*	
Baseball scores	Chamber music by a noted string quartet
Dance music	
Songs by a great ballad singer	
	The whole opera "Cavalleria Rusticana" with explanations
Lecture on the "Wedding Ring, Past and Present"	
A story by a famous author	News of the day
Weather forecast for the following day	

Sales Dept., Suite 2065
233 Broadway
New York, N. Y.

District Office
10 So. La Salle Street
Chicago, Ill.

In 1922, this ad appeared. The Aeriola delivered far less than promised in this advertisement. Even after redesigning, this model was discontinued.

Bob Sanders wrote a column for *The Springdale News* called *Springdalia*. It contained gossip about the happenings around town—mostly up and down Emma Ave.

I was so naive I thought he was giving me a free plug when he wrote this little blurb about my *Let's Talk TV* columns. Actually it was more of a disclaimer. What he was saying was "Don't hold the *News* responsible for anything Bruce might say."

THE NEWS COMES up with another columnist today . . . He's a three-times-a-week guy, and we are wondering if he is going to get smart with us like some other columnist around here have . . . If so, guess there isn't much we can do about it for he is paying for his space . . . It is BRUCE C. VAUGHAN JR., who is buying space to tell you about television, which he claims is here to stay . . . From what we have seen at home on BRYAN WORK'S outfit, he is right . . . So The News comes up with another columnist . . . Let him blow his horn all he wants—we need the dough * * *

SPEAKING OF television . . . Our house has been quite crowded these nights of late . . . Visitors Sunday night were EILEEN NELSON, BILL NELSON, MRS. CLAYPOOL, MR. and MRS. JOE BAILEY and son . . . We were fortunate to see most of the Philadelphia-Los Angeles championship professional football game . . . CLYDE SCOTT was seen on numerous occasions as he caught passes and ran in the game * * *

* * *

LET'S TALK

TELEVISION

By Bruce C. Vaughan Jr.
Bruce's Radio & Television Co.

We were happy to have DON THOMPSON, the program director of KOTV, the Tulsa television station, as a visitor in our home last night. . . . Mr. THOMPSON was in Springdale checking on the reception here. "I heard Springdale was receiving our station," he said. "I could hardly believe it, so I drove over. I still wouldn't have believed it had I not seen it last night. I think your reception here is wonderful."

And a lot of other people think it is wonderful. More sets are being installed daily. KOTV, Mr. Thompson said, has a listening audience now of over 75,000, and it will have its mobile unit in operation within four months. At that time the station will bring midget auto races and baseball games direct from the field. The future is mighty bright for first-class entertainment from KOTV. Mr. THOMPSON also said the station was planning to increase the number of hours per week they will be on the air.

Have YOU checked into the possibility of television in your home? Call us today. We think we know the answer.

—Bruce.

LET'S TALK

TELEVISION

By Bruce C. Vaughan Jr.
Bruce's Radio & Television Co.

In discussing television with various people I have found that there are many points on which people are misinformed. Here are some typical cases:

Can small screen sets give the same picture detail as the large screen receivers?

Yes. The only difference is in the size of the picture.

Do all TV sets turn in regular programs?

No. A TV set gets both the sight and sound broadcast by the television station. If you want to pick up regular radio programs you must get a TV set designed for this.

Has there been any revolutionary new developments recently that should be a part of the set I buy?

No. Features like circular screens, built-in antennas, "day-night screens" may have a slight advantage in cost reduction or performance, but they are not revolutionary.

Will color TV obsolete my set?

ABSOLUTELY NOT! When color arrives, you will be able to receive it.

Will I need an outdoor antenna?

Positively yes. Any set located more than a few blocks from the station needs an outside aerial.

Come in any time for a visit with us. "Let's talk television."

—Bruce.

Don Thompson, a former Rogers businessman, heard of our reception of KOTV and paid us a visit. It was rather amazing that we received KOTV with any degree of regularity. The station was very low power, and the antenna was mounted on the Philtower Building.

Our columns were written by a staff member of the *News*. I would talk, they would listen, then write up the little column. They sometimes lost something in translation. This one is a good example.

My statement was that when color TV arrived, those who owned black-and-white TVs would be able to receive the color programs in black-and-white.

LET'S TALK

TELEVISION

By Bruce C. Vaughan Jr.

Bruce's Radio & Television Co.

I have just returned from Little Rock where I attended the showing of the new 1950 model ADMIRAL television sets at the Albert Pike Hotel. I was amazed at the complete line of television offered, and at the surprisingly low cost of the new model sets.

For instance, did you know you could buy a 12½-inch screen, straight television set for $189.50. This price is for the table model. The price scale ranges upward to $316.95 for a complete radio-record player-television console. Who said a television set-up would cost from $500 to $1,000?

I have all the information regarding these sets available now, and I am ready to talk television with you. We'll check your premises, and we'll be able to tell you whether you will be able to receive television or not. Others are enjoying good television performance—why not you. See us today.

—Bruce.

LET'S TALK

TELEVISION

By Bruce C. Vaughan Jr.

Bruce's Radio & Television Co.

"Fibber" McGhee, mechanic for the Bearcat Service Station, bought a television set from BRUCE RADIO & TELEVISION SHOP a couple of weeks ago. It was one of the first sold in Northwest Arkansas to people other than dealers. A few nights ago I dropped by McGhee's house and watched a television program on how to fish. It is my opinion that McGhee could give some pointers on fishing to the expert we were watching. At least McGhee catches bigger ones than the ones we saw on the television program.

This program was being telecast over KOTV, Tulsa, Oklahoma. This station is now on the air seven nights a week and carried all of the major TV shows.

Contrary to public opinion, the winter season offers the poorest reception. The best reception comes in the summer months.

Remember, we are dealers for ADMIRAL television sets. See us today. We'll prove to you television is in Springdale.

TELEVISION

By Bruce C. Vaughan Jr.

Bruce's Radio & Television Co.

During the past few weeks in this column we have been telling you about television. We are deeply interested in television, and want to acquaint you with this latest entertainment innovation. We have tried to point out to you the advantages of television.

While we want to sell television, we also want to remind you our main stock in trade is radio sales and repair. We are dealers for the fine new 1950 ADMIRAL line of radios. . . . We have a radio for every need, and to fit every pocketbook.

Our repair department is the most complete in this section. Our workmen are experienced.

If you are in the market for a radio, or if you have a radio that needs a repair job—see us today.

—Bruce.

TELEVISION

By Bruce C. Vaughan Jr.

Bruce's Radio & Television Co.

Weather conditions affect television reception. Those who own sets in Springdale can tell you that. Changing conditions usually cause a somewhat ragged picture, and sometimes reception is completely knocked out.

The coming of the present cold wave is a good example. The reception the past few nights hasn't been too good.

We have been frank with all those who have purchased sets or who are thinking of buying a set. You can not expect perfect reception every night. The yearly average, we believe, will be four good nights per week.

Television is somewhat different from radio. In addition to the transmission of the audio waves, the television station must telecast the picture and a number of other waves to stabilize the picture.

Don't expect perfect reception every night. But remember that you can get a clear picture most of the time.

—Bruce.